NLP FOR ENTREPRENEURS

Reprogram Your Entrepreneurial Mind for Better Decision Making, Negotiation Skills and Higher Self-Confidence Using these NLP Techniques to 10X Your Business

Joel E. Winston

4

Hello busy entrepreneur,

To fully master new NLP techniques, scientific studies show, that you need to repeat them several times in different time-frames. This depends on your experience, background and on technique of course.

For your convenience, we have assembled a PDF document with the 26 most important NLP Techniques for you as a busy entrepreneur.

You can print this PDF or parts of this PDF as much as you want. Place the NLP Technique where it´s the most convenient for you. You can choose your bathroom mirror, the fridge in your kitchen or the monitor at your business. Test what works best for your personal situation

If you want to be a productive entrepreneur:

- Go to:
  http://nlpforentrepreneurs.businessleadershipplatform.com/

- Or scan the QR Code

- Get the PDF with the 26 NLP techniques for Entrepreneurs

- Print (parts of) the PDF

- Start applying the NLP Techniques **to 10x your business**

Enjoy!

Joel

Table of Contents

INTRODUCTION 9

CHAPTER 1: NLP EXPLAINED 17

Background 17

A Brief History of NLP 19

Components and Founding Concepts 22

NLP Modeling Explained 23

CHAPTER 2: ENTREPRENEURIAL MISSION/MOTIVATION 29

Getting Motivated 29

Examples of submodalities 32

Visual and auditory submodalities exercise 35

Setting Goals 41

NLP Well-informed Outcome Model 42

The NLP Timeline Model 47

CHAPTER 3: CONFIDENCE 49

Removing Fear 49

NLP Techniques to Overcome Fear 51

Gaining Confidence 58

NLP Techniques for Building Self-confidence 60

NLP Swish Technique 61

NLP Get Grounded Exercise for Boosting Confidence 63

Mommy, Make it Go Away Technique 64

NLP Whiteout Technique 67

NLP Technique to Kill Nagging Voices 68

NLP Anchoring Technique to Gain Confidence 69

CHAPTER 4: SELF-APPRECIATION AND SELF-ESTEEM 73

Self-Appreciation 73

Self-Esteem 75

NLP Ten-Step Self-Esteem Enhancer 78

NLP Seven-Step Self-Esteem Booster   81

The Six-Step Reframing Technique   85

NLP Belief Disintegrator Technique   87

NLP Belief Creator Technique   89

CHAPTER 5: PRODUCTIVITY AND TIME MANAGEMENT   **91**

NLP Visual Squash Technique   94

CHAPTER 6: COMMUNICATION   **97**

Creating and Building Rapport   101

Using Eye Accessing Cues   104

Further reading   **117**

REFERENCES   **119**

INTRODUCTION

We all want success; everyone would like to make more money than they could reasonably spend. Unfortunately, for all our best efforts, more people fail at entrepreneurship than those that succeed. It is not hard to see why, though.

The average entrepreneur is bedeviled by a myriad of challenges, loopholes, and blockades. He is typically the sole decision-maker, planner, and visionary in the business, and his viewpoints and positions on business-related matters usually triumph over others'. Unfortunately, most people are not well equipped to handle this load all by themselves.

Therefore, the entrepreneur needs to be in a state of perpetual mental, emotional, and psychological excellence, so as to be in full capacity to handle their business dealings as meticulously and successfully as achievable. Unfortunately, intrinsic factors effectively hinder entrepreneurs' smooth sail to business success. The four major, personal problems that entrepreneurs encounter are;

(1) Poor time management,

(2) Poor decision-making,

(3) Low self-confidence, and

(4) Bad communication.

These problems make it increasingly difficult for these entrepreneurs to convert hard work and planning into business victory efficiently. Unless they are gotten rid of, or minimized to the barest minimum, productivity continues to suffer.

For instance, many entrepreneurs put a great deal of effort and time into their business, working endless hours every day – including weekends and holidays. Yet, some of these business owners find that the results their efforts are accruing are not congruent with the amount of time they put in. This problem of time management is faced by entrepreneurs across all spheres and sizes of business, although large business owners seem to show a greater proclivity to suffering the strains of poor time management – and more severely – than medium-scale or small-scale business owners. Nevertheless, effective time management is a trait all entrepreneurs must endeavor to have irrespective of their business sector or size. Problems with time management are often caused by factors such as procrastination, distractions, multitasking, failure to prioritize, and ineffectual planning.

Another scourge of the contemporary world of entrepreneurs is the problem of bad decision making. One of the invaluable traits of successful entrepreneurs is their ability to make decisions in the spur of the moment – decisions that very often have the potential to decide the trajectory of their business. In the face of the innumerable everyday hassles that entrepreneurs face in their lines of business, it is vital that they are able to cough out the right major and minor decisions concerning the running of their business quickly and effectively. Failure to make decisions or act on them quickly enough lies at the root of the downfall of many businesses. It is also a major reason why some companies fall short of expectations and/or lose the market to their competitors. Aside from the negative effects that poor decision-making can have on a business, entrepreneurs may suffer the consequences of their bad decisions in their lives; it is not very rare to find a failed entrepreneur exhibiting symptoms of depression.

Low self-esteem and low self-confidence are also factors that impede entrepreneurial progress. Entrepreneurs suffering from low self-esteem usually find it unbearably difficult to respect their workers and customers and seem to over-compensate for their low self-confidence by being overly rude and arrogant. These attitudes often lead to dissatisfaction among workers or team members and a consequent decrease in productivity at the workplace. Hence, such entrepreneurs open themselves up to not only the routine hassles of everyday work, but also the challenge of dealing with co-owners, workers, and customers who perpetually feel belittled and unvalued. This is not the perfect recipe for a successful business outfit.

Even when an entrepreneur has learned to manage time effectively to achieve desired results, has rock-solid self-esteem and confidence to see deals through, and always seems to make the right decisions concerning business matters, poor communication between themselves and team members, customers or clients could still hamper the desired flow of business dealings, thereby impacting negatively on results. Some of the reasons for poor communication are poor listening skills, talking over others, and failing to ask enough or appropriate questions.

The effects of ineffective communication include failure to motivate or inspire team members, poorly presented and understood ideas, poor employee performance, and ineffectual negotiation skills, amongst others. In order to build and sustain a successful business enterprise, entrepreneurs need to be able to communicate clearly through both verbal and non-verbal means. After all, all business dealings with clients, investors, team members, and customers require some sort of communication to run through.

All of these problems that impede an entrepreneurs' path to success can be remedied through the application of Neuro-linguistic Programming (NLP). What is NLP?

NLP is a method of communication and personal development and wellness designed in the 1970s by Richard Bandler and John Grinder to help people achieve certain goals in their lives. The three components of Neuro-Linguistic programming are Neuro, Linguistic, and Programming.

The *Neuro* component describes how every individual uses their unique internal refining system to analyze and understand the multitudes of information they take in through their senses; the *Linguistic* component describes the way the state of mind translates into verbal and non-verbal communication; the *Programming* component identifies one's ability to alter the state of the body and mind.

The concept of NLP takes root in the assumption that there is an interconnection between the body's neurological processes, spoken language, and certain behaviors that have been learned over a period of time, and that these variables can be modified to achieve desired goals and objectives. NLP has also been hypothesized to have a capacity to make ordinary people acquire exceptional skills by modeling the skills of exceptional people. Furthermore, NLP practitioners and experts claim that its methodology can prove useful in the treatment of abnormalities, including phobias, allergy, depression, and near-sightedness.

NLP aims to understand the way people organize their thoughts, emotions, and language. It also tries to observe how these lead to the results that people obtain. In other words, it studies how individuals develop their unique 'maps of the world' according to how they perceive the information they have received from the environment through their senses. NLP teaches not only fluidity in interpersonal communication, but also fluency in communicating with oneself. It literally assists you to communicate better with yourself by teaching you and getting you to master the language of your mind.

Hitherto known as the study of subjective experience, NLP has its roots in the domain of intrapersonal communication and has been used by psychotherapists and specialized NLP practitioners to enable people to understand themselves better and, therefore, make better decisions and live an overall richer and happier life. NLP teaches that you are fully in control of, and can alter, the workings of your mind, to achieve either positive or negative results. Through the help of NLP's techniques, you can learn to gradually reduce and eventually eradicate the negative emotions, feelings, behaviors, and actions that impede your growth and development, and replace them with positive ones that will help plunge your business into an unprecedented success.

There are tons of NLP techniques that can help entrepreneurs improve their thinking, decision making, and performance. These techniques include anchoring, mirroring, Metamodel, framing, pattern interruption, and a whole lot more.

Anchoring is a technique used to put oneself in a particular state of mind. It is useful for oneself or on another person. Anchoring works through the association or linking of emotion with a specific action, a process known as 'laying the anchor.' Mirroring is an NLP technique that you can use to mimic the behaviors of someone you are communicating with. This mimicking, which is usually done subtly, can take the form of copying one's speech, gait, tone, general body language, and speech volume.

The Metamodel technique is useful in developing an understanding of another individual's problems, and to help them understand their problems better. While using the Metamodel NLP technique, you are inadvertently trying to find the root cause of the problem being experienced by an individual with whom you are conversing and to find an effective solution to that problem. The framing technique is employed to increase or reduce emotional feelings. This technique is especially invaluable to entrepreneurs, who typically have to experience a lot of emotions through their engagements with different kinds of people. Pattern interruption NLP technique is another tool used to place words in the subconscious mind of a person you are communicating with. These are just a few of the tens of NLP techniques you can use to bolster your personality and business.

NLP had even been adopted for the treatment of certain mental abnormalities as well as for personal growth and improvement since its inception four decades ago, and its efficacy in bringing about positive results has been supported by scientific research. One study published in the *Counselling and Psychotherapy Research* journal concluded that patients undergoing psychotherapy showed improvement in the quality of life after they were exposed to NLP compared to a group that did not receive NLP therapy. [1] Another research paper, published in 2015, found that NLP has positive effects on patients suffering from psychological or social problems. [2] Though more research is needed in the field of NLP to offer more support to its theoretical framework, the efficacy of its practical application has been proven through improvement in the quality of life of thousands of individuals across the globe.

The application of NLP in your life and business comes with lots of benefits. One of the benefits is that you get better clarity of your vision and purpose. NLP improves offers personal development as it helps you modify your subconscious behaviors to bring about positive results. NLP also gives you more confidence and self-esteem to handle your business dealings optimally and succinctly by helping you to alter and replace your limiting beliefs with more optimistic ones.

In the world of entrepreneurs, you are constantly dealing with people – a lot of people – who come with different personalities, traits, and attitudes. By applying certain NLP techniques, you can learn to manage difficult people, dealing with them in ways that would benefit your business. As an entrepreneur, you are inevitably a leader; your employees, team members, clients, and even customers look to you for support and guidance. NLP can help strengthen your leadership abilities and shape you into a proactive rather than reactive leader. Exposing yourself to NLP can assist you in assessing your present thought, emotional, and behavioral patterns, and creating patterns that are focused on building you to become a problem-solving entrepreneur, thereby increasing your efficiency and performance. Furthermore, NLP techniques help improve your negotiation skills by making you more 'flexible' in communications with clients and customers and potentially increase sales.

NLP has transformed the lives of many people all over the world, turning them into a better version of themselves and helping them to achieve unprecedented success in their respective industries. Tony Robbins, Eben Pagan, and Stefan James Pylarinos, to mention a few, are some of the people who have used NLP to reshape their reality and enterprise. By mastering and applying the concepts of NLP in their lives, they have been able to ascend from humble positions to great heights seamlessly.

Tony Robbins made his first contact with NLP through one of its founders, John Grinder, in the 1980s. He learned several NLP techniques, such as 'firewalk,' which he incorporated into his seminars. By 1991, his infomercials had garnered over 100 million views. He has been named as one of the top 50 business intellectuals by *Accenture*, one of the top 200 business gurus by Harvard Business Press and made the *Forbes Celebrity 100* in 2007.

Eben Pagan learned and has incorporated NLP into his enterprises, which include Cliff's List – an online dating newsletter – and a host of books including *Double Your Dating*, *Advanced Dating Series*, *Meeting Women Online*, and *Deep Inner Game*, and claimed in 2009 that his products and services gross about $30 million per annum. Stefan James Pylarinos is another individual who has learned to channel his knowledge of NLP into his business enterprise. He is currently a 7-figure author and a publishing expert, who has built an empire of wealth through eBook retailing.

NLP is a tested and proven method of quickly turning the tides in your business to achieve favorable results. Its teachings and practice can help bolster your decision-making process, improve your self-esteem and self-confidence, better your negotiating skills, grow your leadership skills, and maximize sales. You can also apply the proven NLP techniques that others have used to accomplish great success by mastering the teachings contained in this book. No matter what sector of business you operate in, the size of your enterprise, or the revenue you rake in annually, there is a lot for everyone in this book. The lessons are practical, direct, and easy to incorporate into your daily life. If you are currently struggling with making sales or dealing with employees, customers, or clients, this is the best book out there at the moment that can help put and keep your life and that of your business on track.

By leaning a few NLP techniques presented in this book, you can quickly turn your business stalemate into a checkmate. So, what are you waiting for? Get into this boat and ride your way to phenomenal success!

CHAPTER 1: NLP EXPLAINED

Background

The foundations of NLP were first introduced in the 1970s in two books co-authored by Richard Bandler and John Grinder, *The Structure of Magic I & II*, which they published in 1975 and 1976, respectively. According to Bandler and Grinder, there exists a connection between an individual's neurological processes, language, and the behaviors they exhibit. The functional basis of NLP is founded on the presupposition that these variables can be altered and reshaped to bring about desired effects or results.

Other major theories of NLP are derived from the works of authors such as Virginia Satir, Milton Erickson, and Fritz Perls, as well as the theories of Gregory Bateson, Alfred Korzybski, Noam Chomsky, and Carlos Castaneda. Of particular interest to Bandler and Grinder were the unique therapy techniques utilized by Satir, Erickson, and Perls, and in the first volume of their book, they claimed that NLP methodology is able to clone those techniques and, indeed, any technique utilized for therapy or otherwise, so that they can be used by anybody. This method of creating models out of an original model is known as codification. In fact, the entire volume 1 of *The Structure of Magic* is dedicated solely to this purpose.

NLP is a method of communicating with the mind. It takes into cognizance that individuals fashion their unique internal maps of the world as they apply a mental filter to the information they receive from their surroundings. NLP helps to achieve resonance with an individual's unique map, so as to understand why and how they do what they do. Away from understanding the thought and behavioral patterns of others, NLP also helps to understand the workings of one's own mind and to communicate vividly with it. Hence, NLP has been described by many as the study of the language of the mind.

Here is an instance to help you understand NLP better. Imagine that you went to an eatery in a foreign country and tried to order a fruit salad in a language you barely understand. After forty minutes of waiting, the steward came with a sandwich. You lividly stormed out of the eatery, frustrated, tired, and most importantly, still hungry. This is potentially very frustrating and might impact negatively on your entire trip. However, the sour experience could have been avoided had you communicated better with the steward. You probably thought you ordered fruit salad, but perhaps in reality, what you asked for was a hamburger.

This instance is similar to the workings of our subconscious mind. Sometimes you feel you are asking for happiness, wealth, and health, but then get stagnation and disease. You begin to think life is unfair, but what you asked for is what you are getting. You simply don't understand the language of your mind. With NLP, you can learn not only to speak but also master the language of your mind.

NLP has been defined in several ways. One such definition describes NLP as the study of communication within oneself and between oneself and other individuals. In this light, NLP has been developed through modeling expert communicators who achieved positive outcomes with their clients. NLP has also been defined as a method of communication, therapy, and personal development, which is aimed at bringing about desired favorable outcomes. Perhaps the most encompassing definition of NLP is that it is a pathway to utilizing the language of the mind to achieve results consistently.

A Brief History of NLP

Although a vast majority of the texts about NLP celebrates John Grinder and Richard Bandler as the founding fathers and originators of NLP, it is worthy to note that several more people were involved in carving out the theories and doctrines of NLP. These remarkable people, including Frank Pucelik, Robert Dilts, Judith Delozier, Leslie Cameron, David Gordon, among others, strove to pave the way for the NLP practiced today.

At the inception of NLP, these individuals, together with Grinder and Bandler, set out on an intellectual mission at the University of California to find out why the techniques employed by exceptional psychotherapists Erickson, Satir, and Perls were so effective on clients. They relied on direct observation of these psychotherapists as they communicated with clients, as well as analyses of their therapy videos to discover the magic behind their communication genius. The process they used to uncover and breakdown the strategies of Erickson, Satir, and Perls is termed modeling, which in essence is creating a copy of what another individual does.

By using the modeling technique, Bandler and Grinder stated in their 1975 book, *The Structure of Magic I* that they could codify the works of individuals who have excelled in their fields and through that codification expose the structure of the strategies employed by those people, thereby making the knowledge available for other people to attain. The authors used this methodology in modeling Virginia Satir, to produce what they termed the *Meta-Model*, a tool for assessing a client's spoken language and discovering the thoughts behind it. Bandler and Grinder claimed that by challenging a client's language, one could be privy to the deeper-lying information usually hidden just beneath the *surface*.

Towards the end of the 1970s, the *human potential movement* became more influential and sprouted in its wake an entire industry, which gave NLP concepts and teachings fertile grounds to grow and flourish. Central to the early development of NLP is the Esalen Institute at Big Sur, California, where renowned psychotherapists including Perls, Satir, and Bateson taught in and led seminars. Circa that time, Bandler and Grinder began to market NLP as not only a therapy option but also a system for communication, and attracted business people by using the mantra, "if anybody can do anything, so can you." They started organizing seminars and workshops to teach therapists and students alike the tenets of NLP. In one of such workshops, they made $150,000 when 150 students paid $1,000 each to attend their 10-day workshop. After that initial success, Bandler and Grinder decided to quit academic writing for the more financially promising niche writing, transforming transcripts from seminars into books. One such book that resulted from this endeavor is *Frogs into Princes*, which sold a remarkable 270,000 copies worldwide. Indeed, certain documents revealed that by 1980, Bandler alone had made a whopping $800,000 from book sales and workshops.

As the days went by, NLP became more popular, evidently through the participation of students and psychotherapists in its training sessions. One of those early participators was Tony Robbins, who learned NLP from Grinder and thereafter incorporated its teachings into his motivational speaking programs. Despite Bandler's several attempts – some legal, others commercial – to cut off other practitioners from using NLP techniques, the practice of NLP continued to grow. As NLP became increasingly widespread in the 1980s, it was greeted with myriads of scientific studies regarding its founding theories and the effectiveness of its practice. The 1990s saw a decline in scientific interest in the theories and applications of NLP, and even more decline was observed in subsequent years.

The combined endeavor of Bandler and Grinder towards the development and sustainability of NLP suffered a major blow when in 1981, Bandler took legal action against Grinder for the latter's purported utilization of NLP and its teachings in commercial activities to personal ends. Bandler won the suit, and as part of the settlement between himself and Grinder, he agreed to give Grinder a 10-year license to use NLP's concepts for financial enterprises, on the condition that he be paid royalties in return.

Years later, in 1996 and 1997, Bandler instituted legal actions against Grinder for a breach of the settlement agreement they had, as well as against more than 200 other individuals for 'illegally' using the NLP brand for personal gains. However, the court ruled against Bandler in 1997, stating that Bandler did not have the right to own NLP and all of its concepts, nor did he possess the exclusive authority to license or certify persons in the practice of NLP. This fallout between the two most famous founding fathers of NLP led to criticism and mockery from the ever-present NLP abhorrers and critics. One of the many criticisms came from Stollznow, who commented in 2010 that the purportedly proven techniques of NLP could not prove effective in settlement of the feud between their developers.

In the late 1990s, NLP garnered wider practice when Tony Clarkson took legal action against Bandler to have his NLP trademark in the United Kingdom revoked. The court ruled against Bandler, revoking his trademark and thereby making NLP more 'open-source.' In the year 2000, Bandler again teamed up with Grinder in a marriage of convenience to agree to be regarded as the co-founders of NLP, and to not instigate any actions intended to impact negatively on either of their ventures concerning NLP. Through all of the legal proceedings that have happened as regards the practice of NLP, membership in, and certification by any society offering NLP services remain unhindered and unrestricted to this day.

It was important to get you up to speed with this background of NLP before we start. It might come in handy for you if you ever have to defend why you have chosen NLP as a tool for self-growth.

Components and Founding Concepts

The teachings of NLP cannot be truly understood without first grasping the underpinning components and concepts that form its foundations. These components are subjectivity, consciousness, and learning.

- **Subjectivity**

As explained by Bandler and Grinder, individuals go through life and perceive information in a subjective manner, thereby creating subjective versions of their experience. In other words, they create unique maps of the world. These mental versions of experience are organized from information gathered from the five senses – eyes, ears, skin, nose, and tongue – as well as the spoken language. This is why when we recall an event that happened in the past, we tend to "see" images of the event, "hear" the sounds that accompanied the event, "feel" the sensations we felt when we experienced the event, "smell" the odors associated with it, "taste" the flavors of the event, and generally think in some language (typically our most preferred language, or one we are most fluent in). Therefore, in light of the structure and pattern of an individual's subjective representations of their experiences, the definition of NLP as a study of the architecture of subjective human experience is credible, logical, and, in fact, laudable. By taking into account the subjectivity of ours and people's perception of information, we can understand behaviors – why we do what we do –, and by modifying the subjective representations of experiences, we can successfully and consistently alter behaviors both in ourselves and in others.

- **Consciousness**

According to the teachings of NLP, the concept of consciousness can be divided into two individual components: the conscious component and the unconscious component. The conscious component comprises conscious thoughts, actions, emotions, and behaviors, while the unconscious component includes all of an individual's subjective representations of their experiences.

- **Learning**

NLP is predicated on the concept of learning through imitation, also called modeling, whereby an exceptional person's skills and mastery in a field or art can be codified and replicated for use by other people.

NLP Modeling Explained

Modeling is arguably the handiest skill in Neuro-linguistic Programming. It is the sum total of the methods involved in the recreation of exceptional strategies employed by individuals to achieve excellent outcomes, for the purpose of allowing other people 'copy' those strategies to achieve similar outcomes. The modeling concept is founded on the notion that any human behavior or strategy can be modeled by carefully assessing, understanding, and mastering the beliefs, skills, and thought patterns associated with that behavior. In other words, it is simply putting yourself in the shoes of the individual whose behavior you want to model. Modeling is like burning a program from a computer, A, onto a compact disc, and then installing that program on another computer, B, that did not have it so that it can begin to run the program too.

It is essential to think of modeling not as an instruction manual, but as a tool that can be used to 'hack' into the strategies of successful endeavors. It is vital, therefore, that before you set out to use modeling, you ascertain what it is you want to achieve, and then open yourself up to the possibility of getting one of several possible outcomes. The goals of NLP modeling include helping you develop skills, behaviors, and strategies that are aimed toward improving your performance, assessing behaviors so that you know which ones are bad or good to keep, and getting to understand other people better so as to create rapport. The processes involved in achieving these goals come in three phases:

a. First phase: Model observation

In this phase, the modeler (you, in this case), attempts to imagine themselves in the state and reality of the individual they are trying to model (also called the model) by employing a term called *second position shift*. Here, you must try to focus on the things the model does (this includes behaviors and physiology), how they achieve these (what thought patterns they have while doing the things they do), and why they do it (their belief systems, assumptions, and presuppositions). You can ascertain what the model is doing by directly observing them; how and why they do those things can be deduced by asking them questions and carefully assessing their feedbacks.

b. Second phase: Yanking out the difference

This phase involves finding out the essential ingredient in the model's strategy. Modeling allows us to take out all of a model's characteristics or elements and assess each one to find out which one makes the difference. By trying out element after element, the model's strategy should fail to work without the essential element. Therefore, the element, without which the strategy does not have value, or does not produce the desired effects, is *the difference*. To arrive at a probable result, you must endeavor to ask quality questions, such as:

- What behaviors does the model exhibit?
- How does the model achieve their results?
- What did the model do differently than other strategies that did not achieve success?
- What is *the difference*?

c. Third phase: Teaching the strategy

This is the final phase of the modeling process. When you have found out and mastered a model's strategy and all of its elements, you would then be in a position to teach others the vital skill the model is using to achieve their exceptional results.

The above-detailed phases of modeling can be further broken down into simpler steps, for practicability and easier comprehension. These are:

1. Ascertain the exceptional individual you want to model. Ensure that you have seen them perform the skills you want to model, either firsthand or in a videotape. Watch and listen to them as they perform the skills as many times as feasible.
2. Get yourself in a comfortable position, usually sitting, and then try to imagine the model performing the skill. Try as much as possible to imagine yourself getting in sync with them as they perform.
3. Imagine 'getting into' the model's body as they perform the skill. You have to be creative in your imagination, as you try to feel, hear, and see what they feel, hear, and see as they perform the skill.
4. 'Get back' into your body, and as you do that, make sure you are leaving the model's body with the knowledge you have acquired. Now try to re-imagine the performance of the skill, but now with you as the actor.

5. Repeat step 4 over and over until you are satisfied with your performance.
6. Break the chain, that is, try to focus on something else. For example, you could focus on the ceiling or floor, and observe their designs.
7. Repeat all of the steps above and continue to practice until you have mastered the skill.

The above exercise details the steps involved in modeling another person. But NLP modeling can also be used to model your behaviors. Here is an exercise that can help you model a behavior (such as smoking) and replace it with a better behavior (such as drinking a glass of water instead).

1. Identify the behavior you wish to modify (in this case, say you want to alter your smoking habit).
2. Point out the steps you take to accomplish that behavior.
3. Identify and assess the factors that trigger that behavior.
4. Start making little changes to the steps that get you to accomplish the negative behavior. For example, it may be that you are tempted to smoke whenever you see a cigarette. In this case, seeing a cigarette is the trigger, and now you want to change the result of that trigger, which is lighting and smoking the cigarette and replace it with a healthier behavior, like drinking a glass of water.
5. Use the *future pace* technique to change the result of the trigger. You can do this by imaging that in the future when you see a cigarette, you take it, examine it, and then throw it in the bin. Then you smile and drink a glass of water.
6. Test your imagination. Get a cigarette and a glass of water, then throw the cigarette in the bin and drink the glass of water. Tell yourself that it is ACTUALLY easier and better to drink the glass of water instead of smoking.

NLP has proven to be an effective solution to a wide range of problems and bottlenecks. It has been used by practitioners to remedy or, at least, minimize the symptoms of low self-esteem, depression, certain phobias, and more. It is because of its possible applications in these diverse areas that NLP has garnered the amount of fame and widespread practice it currently enjoys. Over the last four years of its existence, NLP has been used by psychotherapists and other practitioners to bring about better communication, smoother customer relations, and other positive outcomes in the businesses of entrepreneurs. It helps improve your interpersonal skills.

Effective communication is central to the concept of NLP and is a key fixture in most NLP techniques and strategies. Communication is not only words, as the unspoken cues in a conversation, such as eye movement and body postures can often tell the rationale or reasoning behind spoken words, and therefore form the bulk of communicated language. NLP can teach you to become a master of nonverbal communication, so that you better understand the 'why' behind the 'what' in communications with clients, customers, and team members. Through modeling, NLP allows you to replicate the strategies that successful enterprises have utilized to their benefit and achieve similar levels of success to what they attained. NLP improves negotiation skills so that you can close deals more easily and successfully too.

In this chapter, I have tried to bring you up to speed with the formation and development of NLP as a widely accepted and adopted technique. The core tenets have also been introduced to you. This background is important as we now move to localize NLP techniques to entrepreneurship in subsequent chapters.

CHAPTER 2: ENTREPRENEUR-IAL MISSION/MOTIVATION

Getting Motivated

Motivation is the fuel of success. A motivated individual is an individual driven and pushed by the desire to succeed. Unfortunately, with the weight of everyday struggles bearing down on us, it may be difficult to be perpetually motivated. While NLP has been used over the years mainly to offer solutions to psychological anomalies such as phobias, depression, and compulsive disorders like (binge eating disorder), some of its techniques have also proven useful as a means of motivating people.

One of the most common techniques used to induce motivation is modeling. The concept of modeling, including its theory and practical application, has been discussed in the previous chapter. In light of motivation, you can use modeling to model an individual who seems to have the ability to stay motivated by assessing the behaviors and thought patterns that enable them to achieve that level of motivation.

Another NLP technique that is used for motivational purposes is that of 'copying' a skill or resource that an individual has and installing it in another person. Think of the compact disk example given in chapter 1! A motivation strategy can be installed in an individual in one of several ways:

- Using a strategy elicitation technique to copy a motivational strategy from an individual and installing it on yourself or another person,

- Using a strategy that worked for you in the past or that you currently use to get motivated for a task, or
- Developing a motivational strategy of your own from scratch.

Since the first option is inextricable similar to the modeling technique we have learned and tested earlier, we will not delve further into it. The second option tends to be the preferred option for most people as it is considered the easiest of the three. I am therefore going to demonstrate how you can reuse a strategy you used in the past to motivate you to carry out a task in the present. But you cannot truly understand the technique involved in this strategy without first getting familiar with *submodalities*. So, what is meant by the term submodalities?

Submodalities, as the term implies, are the subsets (*sub-)* of the sensations – visual, auditory, olfactory, gustatory, and kinesthetic – (*modalities*) through which we fashion and give shape to our experiences. In simpler terms, submodalities are the bricks with which we 'build-up' our experiences. In the early days of NLP, submodalities were used as a way to give color to experiences. However, in 1983, Richard Bandler started to offer an explanation of the nature and architecture of submodalities. He showed how people could use *submodality shifts* to alter their habits, modify beliefs, and induce motivation, and how the root structure of experiences could be revealed using the principles of submodalities.

A submodality as regards NLP can be defined as a distinction or variation in a sensory modality, as perceived by an individual. In other words, submodalities are the subjective 'shades' of the structures of the sensory representational systems. The concept of submodalities in NLP is predicated on the notion that humans fashion experiences using some or all of their five senses. The five senses, including eyes (visual sensation), ears (auditory sensation), skin (kinesthetic sensation), nose (olfactory sensation), and tongue (gustatory sensation), are called the modalities or *representational systems* in NLP.

The principle of submodalities comprises the finer details to each of

The representational systems

these modalities. For example, a substance could be described as sweet or bitter in taste or described as strong or sour. An image could be light or dark, or low or high in contrast. An odor can be pungent or mild, or pleasant or unpalatable. These distinctions or variations are known as submodalities and represent the structure of the internal workings of our minds. NLP submodalities have been used as a standalone technique, in conjunction with other techniques, or incorporated into therapy strategies to help individuals quit smoking, modify their dietary behaviors, challenge compulsive disorders, scrutinize beliefs and highly held values, get motivated, relieve stress, and address phobias.

Examples of submodalities

VISUAL	AUDITORY	KINESTHETIC
Bright or Dim	Mono or Stereo	Heavy or Light
Distant or Close	Low Pitch or High	Rough or Smooth
Color or Black&	Pitch	Warm or Cold
White	Low Volume or High	
Moving or Station-	Volume	
ary		
3D or Flat		
Internal or External		

Submodalities play a very important functional role in the mind, as they help project memories and thoughts from the unconscious to the conscious mind. Even though there are literally tons of submodalities, NLP experts hypothesize that certain submodalities are more vital and can bring about weightier effects than the others. It is of vital importance to understand that submodalities differ between individuals, as a result of the subjectivity of the process through which they are formed in every individual, and the particular sets of submodalities inherent to an individual can often be discovered through inquisition and observation.

When a person alters the constitution of their 'vital' submodalities, they are almost always certain to get an immediate change in the way the emotions attached to those submodalities present themselves. Therefore, submodalities provide a unique panacea for therapy, by which we can understand how the mind subjectively structures events or experiences. The concept of submodalities has gained extensive usage in many NLP techniques, including the

Swish technique, Mapping Across, Compulsion Blowout, and NLP treatment of phobias. Let's quickly dive into the Swish technique.

The Swish technique is an NLP method used to alter an undesired behavior in oneself or in others easily and without the need to be overly disciplined. It involves changing one's identity from the person who does the undesired behavior to one who does not. By altering your reality in this manner, you can quickly transform yourself from who you are to who you want to be. After all, we hardly deal with reality as it is, but through our subjective projections of it. That is to say, we deal with life not as it ACTUALLY is, but as we see it. Therefore, by changing the way we perceive reality, we can change outcomes from undesirable to desirable ones. Here is an exercise in learning and using the Swish technique to change an undesired behavior (such as eating chocolate late into the night):

1. Ascertain the trigger(s) for that behavior. For example, you may feel like eating chocolate while watching a movie late into the night, but this trigger is not there in the daytime. Here, the trigger is the time of the day.
2. Develop a mental image of the trigger. Have a picture of say 1:00 am on the clock in your mind.
3. Identify the vital submodalities in that mental picture. For example, think about what makes the picture less attractive. Try reducing the brightness, changing it from color to black & white, changing its size or shape, or making it more distant.
4. Fashion an image of yourself without this undesired behavior. What would you look like without the habit you are trying to quit? Would you look and feel healthier? Would you have whiter teeth? Would you stop having digestion problems and therefore feel more comfortable in the mornings?
5. Identify the vital submodalities in this desirable mental picture of yourself. Make it more attractive by tweaking certain submodalities. Try bringing it nearer, making the colors

more vivid and bright, increasing the size of the image, or adding background music.

6. Check if you agree with this desirable mental picture. Do you have any worries concerning how this desirable image might affect your life?

7. Now, bring the two mental images side by side, or make them overlap, whichever works for you, but make the undesired image large, colorful, and attractive while leaving the desired image small, bland, and unattractive.

8. Quickly explode the desired image into a large, attractive image and simultaneously shrink the undesired image into a small, distasteful picture while making a swiiiiissssshhhh sound. Allow this new image to linger for a few seconds to savor its beauty.

9. Break state. You can stare at the ceiling or floor or use any other method you are comfortable with. It is important to break the state as you do not want to swish back to the former image.

10. Quickly repeat steps 5 to 9 at least four times.

11. Test. See if thinking about the undesirable image immediately brings the desirable image.

Now that we have a decent understanding of what submodalities are and why they are important in NLP, let's slide back to option two of how to install a motivation strategy via the following steps:

1. The first thing to do is to create a mental image of an action or behavior that you do without much effort, such as brushing your teeth or taking a shower.

2. Then, create a mental image of the thing you want to be motivated to do.

3. Using table 2.2, fill the visual and auditory submodalities of the thing you usually do effortlessly in the 'Motivated To Do' column and those of the thing you want to be motivated to do in the 'Not Motivated To Do' column.

Visual and auditory submodalities exercise

VISUAL		
Submodality	**Motivated To Do**	**Not Motivated To Do**
Brightness (Bright or Dim)		
Position (Near or Far)		
Size (Large or Small)		
Color (Black & White or Color)		
Focus (Blurred or Sharp)		
Distance (Close or Distant)		
Movement (Moving or Stationary)		
Border (With border or Panoramic)		
Associated (Seeing it through your eyes or Seeing yourself in the image)		

AUDITORY		
Submodality	**Motivated To Do**	**Not Motivated To Do**
Volume (Quiet or loud)		
Tone (High or Low tone)		
Tempo (Slow or Fast)		
Pitch (High or Low pitch)		
Direction (What direction is the sound coming from?)		

The aim of table 2.2 is to enable you to figure out the differences in the submodalities between the task you do with ease and that which you need to be motivated to carry out.

4. Now that you have successfully listed the submodalities associated with these tasks use this table as a template and create a similar, blank table. List the differences in the submodalities between the two tasks, disregarding the similarities.

5. Once you have figured out the difference between the submodalities, the next step is to identify the vital submodalities altering, which can create that feeling of motivation. To do this, you will have to 'match' the submodalities of the task you are unable to be motivated to do with those of the task you feel easily motivated to do. For example, if the motivated image had loud music playing in the background, but the unmotivated image had quiet music or none at all, change the unmotivated image so that it now has loud music playing in the background. If the motivated image was a panoramic im-

age and the unmotivated image had a thick, black border around it, change the unmotivated image to a panoramic image. Every time you change a submodality in the unmotivated image, observe how you feel about the new image, then remove the change. Do this for each of the differences in the submodality between the motivated image and the unmotivated image until you find the submodality that makes the difference.

6. Once you have discovered the vital submodality, apply the change to your mental image of the task you are unmotivated to do.

7. Break state. You can stare at the ceiling or floor or use any other method you are comfortable with. It is important to break the state as you do not want to swish back to the former image.

8. Visualize the new image of the task again, and then break state. Repeat this until the new image becomes the primary image you see when you think of the task you were feeling unmotivated to perform.

9. Take a breather.

10. Think of the task you were hitherto feeling unmotivated to do. You should feel differently about it by now. If you are still unmotivated to do it, repeat this exercise.

11. If it still fails to work, try a different set of motivated/unmotivated mental images.

Now let's slide into the third option of installing a motivational strategy, which is making one from scratch.

To create your unique motivational strategy, you need to have a solid understanding of your submodalities. Good knowledge of your submodalities would give you the capability to answer pertinent questions pertaining to the submodalities that motivate you and those that can enhance your attachment to something. As an example, if by making the image of a chocolate bar distorted and small, you can demotivate yourself from eating chocolate, then the opposite should most certainly motivate you. You could also try to identify what auditory submodalities motivate you. For example, if you like a loud, high pitch, female voice behind you telling you to jump at your task and do it, you may wish to try that out – you could get an actual female with these characteristics to do the trick, or imagine it all on your own!

You may also want to incorporate a certain feeling into your motivational strategy. The trick is, if the other submodalities are tuned correctly, the feeling might come naturally. But if it does not, then you would have to use a certain desirable feeling you had some time in the past. Once you have all of the necessary 'ingredients' in their appropriate amounts, installing the strategy is usually easy. All you have to do is keep the feeling, and bring the image to your mind, then tweak the submodalities until you have the desired outcome.

Strategy installation can also be done systematically – following a step-by-step process of instructions. There are at least five different ways in which you can install a new strategy. These are anchoring, accessing cues, repetition, future pace, and metaphor. While you could use any of the five systems to install your brand-new strategy, using a combination of all five has been proven to be more effective in bringing about a positive outcome.

i.   Anchoring

Anchoring, as the name suggests, is a method of 'chaining' a number of sequential steps in a strategy together. When a number of steps have been anchored, you can then 'fire the anchor,' meaning to reverse all of the steps quickly. To make this more interesting, you could inculcate physical movement in the anchor by moving parts or all of your body in a forward direction as you move from step to step in the strategy.

ii.   Accessing Cues

This method is used to associate specific gestures or body movements with steps in a strategy. They are great to use with anchors. For example, as you move your body forward while taking a step in a strategy, you can look to the right to associate that step with the 'eyes-right' accessing cue.

iii.   Repetition

Repetition is an effective way of learning a new habit, skill, or behavior. You can literally repeat the steps in your strategy over and over until you begin to perform them subconsciously.

iv.   Future pace

You could also future pace yourself a number of times upon mastering and applying your strategy.

v.   Metaphor

Metaphors are effective in associating with a strategy. Try using an appropriate metaphor to illustrate your strategy so that you buy into it.

These techniques will be explained in detail in subsequent chapters. It should be incredibly easy to use any or all of these techniques to get motivated for any task you may wish to perform. However, if you still find yourself experiencing bottlenecks in the understanding or application of the techniques and methods herein, you may find solace from adhering to the following tips, as they are designed to help make your self-motivating endeavor a lot less stressful.

- Prioritize. Sometimes the thought of having so much to do can be overwhelming and may discourage you from attempting to do anything at all. Pen down all that you want to do and then pick the top thing you want to accomplish. It may be tempting to try to do so much at a time – multitasking, if you may – but the drawback to this is that you are unable to give every task your best, as they each take only a fraction of your efforts and resources. Focus on one thing at a time, and only move on to another task when you're done and satisfied with the one in hand.

- Outline specifically. You need to make the outcomes of completing a task as specific and detailed as possible. Your mind is the forerunner of your internal affairs, and if it does not have enough clarity as to the benefits you stand to accrue from performing a particular task, it may shut down positive emotions and stifle any urge you may have to perform the task.

- Get away from harm. Picture the cost of not performing the task. How would it impact your business, career, or health? Imagine that a year has passed and you still have not performed that task. How negatively has your failure to perform the task affected that future? Now picture yourself in 3 years still living with the cost of having not done the task. Does that future look bright? Is it what you would have wished for? Chances are, the more unpalatable or unfavorable the cost of not performing a task is, the more motivated you would be to get it done. This is called the "away from" motivation.

- Move toward benefits. You have a vivid mental picture of what your life would be if you don't complete the task you are feeling unmotivated to perform. Now try to picture the benefits of performing that task. How would it affect your life, business, or career in the present, in the near future, and in the distant future? Would it pave the way for you to attain better health, fatter paychecks, or larger clientele? The "toward" motivation, a direct opposite of the "away from" motivation, assumes that the greater the benefits you stand to gain from performing a task, the more your motivation to carry it out would be.

- Less is more. You should endeavor to spend most of your time performing your 'big' tasks rather than the small ones that would yield underwhelming results. Chances are, you have already graded your tasks by the degree of influence in your life and business. But if by chance you have not, you can do so by simply putting them through two filters:
  - o The cost filter: Ask yourself, "How greatly would my not performing this task affect my life, business, relationships, or career? Is it really worth all the time it requires?"
  - o The benefit filter: Ask yourself, "What benefits could completing this task possibly offer? How would these benefits impact my life, business, or career?"

An objective assessment would certainly reveal which tasks have the greatest impact and which ones are simply bugs.

Setting Goals

Goal setting is the cornerstone of all success. It is disheartening than that most people either do not set tangible, specific goals or fail to stay true to them. Whichever is the cause, the outcome remains the same – people who fail to set or stick to their goals end up laboring for those who don't.

In the entrepreneurial world, goal setting has a massive place as regards personal development and business growth. There are many benefits attached to setting goals, and chances are you already know quite a bunch of them. Rather than talk about what you stand to gain from setting goals – which you might already have known – let's take a look at HOW to set goals and stick to them until you eventually achieve them.

There are many models and methods of goal setting employed by people who have attained success in their endeavors. Some of these methods are specific to particular niches and personality types, while others are more general and encompassing. NLP has again come to the rescue to offer effective solutions in the area of goal setting. Perhaps the best NLP models of goal setting applicable to the life of an entrepreneur are the Timeline and Well-Formed Outcome models.

NLP Well-informed Outcome Model

The well-formed outcome model is an NLP technique fashioned from the lives of successful individuals. It involves making an inquiry about your goals and is focused on clarifying your thought patterns and behaviors, on making your goals 'well-formed'. The steps involved in the well-formed outcome model include the following.

1. Clarify the outcome of your goal

It is crucial to have an understanding of the structure of goals. Goals are defined representations of what it is we want in life in our internal environment and, so, must have defined structures as well. Since your mind pretty much controls your emotions and your emotions control your actions, you need to have the correct representations of your goals in your mind in order to be able to achieve them as efficiently as is possible.

The SMART and PURE acronyms are two incredibly useful tools that can help you fashion your goals in a manner that would allow for the optimization of the techniques and methods you employ to achieve them. You need to make your goals SMART and PURE before you can set out to program them into your mind.

- **SMART**

The SMART acronym is based on the goal-setting method developed by Edwin Locke and is described as follows:

- **S** stands for Specific: You need to make your goals as specific as possible, for easier 'assimilation' by your mind. It is much easier to pursue a specific goal that has a definite form than a general one that has tentacles in every direction. While attempting to make your goals specific, you must ensure to ask these invaluable questions:
  o What is it that I want to achieve?
  o With whom do I want to achieve this?
  o When do I want to achieve this?
  o Where would I want to achieve it?
  o What do I require to achieve it?
  o With whom, where, and when do I not want to achieve it?

  The aim of these questions is to give form to your goal, so you can picture it in as vivid a way as possible.

- **M** stands for Measurable: Develop a strategy for measuring your progress towards the achievement of your goal. By tracking your progress, you would be able to stay focused and not detail from the path you have set out to take. Furthermore, measuring your progress gives you the satisfaction of having succeeded thus far in working towards your goal and motivates you to move even further. The caveat to this is, not all goals are measurable. So, from the start, make sure you set out to achieve a measurable goal. You can be certain that your goal is measurable if you can answer the questions of "how much," "how many," and/or "what markers would notify me of progress."

- **A** stands for Attainable: How achievable is the goal you have set out to achieve? Is it extraordinarily huge and illogical for the timeframe? Has it been done by any other person? Although it is a core belief in NLP that one can achieve almost anything one wishes to achieve, it follows logic and reason that you streamline your goals to fit your reality, and. It may be deemed illogical, for instance, for you to have a goal of going to Mars in the next month, while you're currently a small business owner with no affiliations with NASA.

- **R** stands for Relevant: Are your goals relevant to your personal development, business, career, or relationships?

- **T** stands for Timely: What is the timeframe of achieving your goals? By time-binding your goal, you give it a sort of an expiry date, by which you should have attained it.

- **PURE**

PURE is another goal forming method, created by Roger Terry to help clarify your goals and give them meaning.

- **P** means Positive: You must state your goals as though you have already attained them, rather than stating them as if attaining them is not in your capacity.

- **U** means Under Your Control: Get a goal that is entirely or mostly under your control, not a goal the controlling and influencing factors of which is not in your control. For example, "I want to complete the cycling circuit three times in under an hour" would be a better formed goal than "I want to be one of the first three people to complete the circuit three times," because while completing the circuit three times in an hour is under your control, the skills and strength of the other competitors, as well as the number of competitors that enter into the competition, may not be under your control.

- **R** means Right Size: Do you have right-sized goals? Are they too easy to pull off? Are they too difficult to achieve? What is your track record as per achieving set goals?

- **E** means Ecological: What effects would be attaining your goals have on yourself, other individuals, and your relationships with them?

2. Assess your present condition

Even when your goals satisfy all of the SMART and PURE conditions, you might still end up not attaining them because of your current state. You need to assess your condition objectively to identify what it is that is delaying the attainment of your goals. Are you capable of achieving your goals? Do you have the requisite skills, resources, time, and behaviors to achieve them? Sometimes you need to modify a habit or two in order to be in a better position to attain your goals. If you discover that the factors stopping you from achieving your goals are not within your power to control, then let go of those goals and move on. Assume, for example, that you have owned a small toy shop for two years as your sole business and your yearly net profit is $50,000, having a goal to purchase a million-dollar mansion by cash next year might not be achievable, so long as you do not have cash stashed somewhere. In this case, your present condition cannot satisfy the financial demands of buying the mansion.

3. Develop a solid internal representation of your goals

The brain is not as clever as we think it is; it usually cannot discern between real events and imagined or constructed images, as it reacts almost the same way to all of them. Therefore, by creating a strong internal representation of your goals, you help yourself tap into the emotional responses favorable to achieving them. You will have to optimize your use of submodalities in order to create a good internal representation. Use the visual, auditory, and kinesthetic representational systems appropriately to create mental pictures that move you towards attaining your goals. For example, if your goal is to hit the one million dollar net profit mark from your business next year, create a profound mental picture of the goal – using clear images, crisp sounds, and lucid feelings. How would you SEE the one-million-dollar profit? What sounds would you HEAR when you achieve that goal? Do you hear your employees cheering and congratulating one another? How would it FEEL? You need to be able to use appropriate submodalities to construct images of your goal.

4.   Develop a well-formed outcome

This step allows you to assess your progress towards attaining your goals as well as check whether or not they have been completely achieved. These questions should help you in creating a well-formed outcome.

-    What are the markers that will let you know that you have achieved your goal? What will you see, hear, or feel?
-    Do you need other people to help attain your goal?
-    What resources do you require?
-    How will achieving your goal impact your life in general?
-    What effects does achieving your goal have on your life?
-    What effects do not achieve your goal have on your life?

5.   Incorporate your well-formed outcome into your internal representations

Now that you have created a strong internal representation of what you want to achieve and developed a well-formed outcome, it is time to integrate your well-formed outcome into your internal representation, to give you a taste of what it would be like to achieve your goal. Play the scene in your mind several times and travel in its glory. Then, start taking the steps necessary for the attainment of your goal. Use table 2.3 to make taking action about your goal easier for yourself. Write out the first three **actions,** you need to take to attain your goal, **how** you wish to perform them, and **when** you need to get them done. Start with the first action you must take. It could be, for example, putting a call through to a potential investor or customer. Don't make the actions bogus, uninteresting, or unnecessarily complex; make each action ' short', practical, and achievable within a relatively short period of time.

Table 2.3: Action plan to achieve a goal

S/N	ACTION	HOW	WHEN
1.			
2.			
3.			

The NLP Timeline Model

Another effective method of planning or setting a goal is by using the NLP timeline model. The concept of timeline in NLP describes time as a continuum, that is, as a 'stretch' of the reality of our experiences, or, more commonly, a line. Everything that has happened in the past, whatever it is that is happening at present, and everything that will occur in the future are all lined up in a straight line in our minds, such immediate reality (in the past or future) is nearer and distant reality (in the past or future) is farther from the focal point (the present). Another way of picturing time is to take a wall clock and stretch it out so that it makes a straight line. As time goes by, we would be literally 'walking' in a forward direction along the clock line, leaving behind the hours that have come and gone. The entire timeline model, as used in NLP, is founded on this concept of time.

Now that we've understood what timeline is and how it relates to time let's run through the process of setting a goal by using the timeline. This process is broken down into the following steps:

1. Have a mental image of the goal you want to achieve. Make sure to fixate on that image for as long as it would be necessary to ensure that whenever you think of your goal, that image jumps at you.
2. Ascertain the specific time you want to achieve the goal.
3. Picture yourself accomplishing the goal. Be sure to include the visual, auditory, and kinesthetic submodalities necessary to create a solid internal representation.
4. Now, levitate your body in the mental picture.
5. Picture your timeline stretched out in front of you. Holding the mental picture of your goal in your preferred hand, float along your timeline until you reach that specific date and time by which you wish to achieve your goal.
6. Drop the picture at this time and make sure it fits well into it.
7. Float back along your timeline and land on the present time.
8. Break state. You can stare at the ceiling or floor or use any other method you are comfortable with. It is important to break the state as you do not want to swish back to the former image.

You have successfully dropped a goal in the future. Now all you have to do is work towards achieving it. Refer to table 2.3 to kick-start the process.

CHAPTER 3: CONFIDENCE

Removing Fear

This chapter deals with confidence, but before we even mention it, we need to start from its greatest adversary which is fear. Fear is one of the mind's natural responses to a stimulus that does or threatens to cause harm, pain, or endanger our wellbeing. Many people have one, two, or a few things they are scared of – some people have a fear of needles and other sharp, pointed metals; some fear tight places and corners, some have a fear of height, and so forth.

Research has shown that a sizable number of people suffer from one fear or another. Therefore, fears, in general, are not what you would typically describe as weird or abnormal. They are perfectly normal and might even prove beneficial sometimes. A fear of sharp, pointed metal ends, for example, can help us better protect ourselves from needle pricks, which in their own rights are an exceedingly potent way of contracting diseases and infections.

However beneficial they might be, fears have their downsides. They have a capacity to prevent us from driving hard enough towards the attainment of our goals or reduce our productivity and efficiency at the workplace. In the entrepreneurial world, the commonest kind of fear that cripples entrepreneurs and reduces their vigor and steadfastness in pursuing and achieving business successes **is the fear of failure**.

Failure has become an 'unheard-of' sort of result in the society. Nobody likes to fail or even think about the possibility of them failing in an endeavor. The thought of failure seems overwhelming. But it is a possibility; and because we know it is always there waiting by the corner, we always seem afraid of it popping out its head from the shadows. Unfortunately, when the fear of failure is allowed to grow over time, it becomes suffocating, confining, and stagnating. It hinders you from taking the sorts of activities that can help you and your business grow. It becomes a limiting, self-imposed barrier.

Mostly when people look back on the lives they have lived and the things they have done, they regret not the repercussions of what they did, but the things they should have done but failed to do. In essence, people tend to regret their inaction more than their actions. In that case, it is vital to remove any fear of failure that is hindering you from pursuing your goals. Here are some ways that a fear of failure can harm you as an entrepreneur:

- Fear of failure cripples, limits, and restricts you. By being afraid to fail, you are deeply inclined to playing it safe and avoiding any major risks. You avoid at all costs any endeavor that might have the capacity to break you free from your current level and plunge you into a higher level of success. As a result of the deep-seated fear, you are inadvertently forced to see only the possible harmful outcomes that may result from an action, rather than the benefits you're likely to gain from it. This behavior stagnates your business or at least limits it to minimal growth.

- It makes you resist taking a path that leads to abundance – abundance in wealth, time, and confidence. Though the well-traveled road is usually the easier one, it often leads to a land where there are more people competing for resources than there are resources to cater for them all. People who do not fear failure take the less-traveled path, because they know it often leads to a land where there are fewer people competing for abundant resources.

- It hinders you from expanding. Sometimes, the business might be running smoothly and efficiently, and you might be handling your affairs in a decent way. But if you are operating a business that has seemed to reach its peak success, you would need to expand and explore other possibilities. Fear of failure prevents you from doing this. It tells you to stay put in your little comfort zone and reap all of the booties therein.

This hampers further growth and sophistication of your business practices.

In addition to the points raised above, the fear of failure can impede your ability to make more money, by cutting you off the pathways that lead to wealth creation and growth. It could also impact your personal space, your life. When you refuse to venture into taking actions and exhibiting behaviors that can improve the state of your business, soon, your business stagnates. Once this happens, you begin to develop certain negative emotions such as regrets, depression, and even more fear. These can have severe negative effects on your wellbeing.

NLP Techniques to Overcome Fear

NLP has described many techniques for quickly and effectively removing fears and phobias alike. Some of these techniques were developed by the creators of NLP and others were developed by contributors such as experts in psychotherapy, hypnotherapy, and commercial self-help ventures. Three techniques for overcoming fear are detailed in this chapter. You can attempt all and choose the one(s) that work(s) for you best. Central to almost all NLP techniques to rid oneself of fear lies the concept of anchoring. To understand these techniques then, you must first gain an understanding of what anchors are and how they are used in NLP.

-   **What are Anchors?**
Anchoring is one of the most commonly utilized NLP techniques, largely due to its effective and rapid impact. It allows you to put yourself in any state you desire consciously – states of happiness, confidence, motivation, etc. – quickly. Anchors have a dual application, that is, they can be applied to oneself or other people. They can be used in the immediate as well as some time in the future. Therefore, in essence, anchors, when they have been developed, are always available on demand.

- How Can Anchors be used?

Anchors are specifically created to bring about a positive change in thought, attitude, or behavior. For example, anchors can be used to evoke positive emotions whenever you see or think about something that usually scares you. In order to be able to create powerful, effective anchors, you need to have a solid understanding of NLP submodalities and how to apply them. Powerful internal representations breed powerful anchors. If you do not create strong enough internal representations, your anchors might be loose and largely ineffective. Mostly, people prefer to use the sense of touch to set up anchors, as they tend to be more accessible than visual or auditory anchors. However, you could also create powerful visual and auditory anchors, as long as you perform the anchoring process conscientiously. Let's dive into an example to make the understanding of anchors easier.

We are going to make an example of how to use NLP anchors to rid ourselves of fear of cockroaches.

- First, think of a time when you were in a state of fearlessness.
- If it so happens that there was not a time in the past you felt fearless, then try to imagine what it would feel like to be fearless.
- Create a vivid mental picture of you being fearless. This could be the day you started your business, the day you had your best presentation or any other moment in your life, you felt no fear whatsoever.
- Once you have that image on your mind, add the appropriate visual and auditory submodalities to make it even more appealing. 'Appropriate' in this sense means the submodalities that make the image more attractive to you. Also, notice the way you feel about the image. For example, if the picture you have in your mind is the day you had your best presentation, try making it colorful, then add your favorite background music. Does the image look better? Is it more appeal-

ing? What you are doing is trying to achieve as strong a mental state as you can develop.

- Keep the feeling building through your body by fixating the mental image to your mind.
- As the feeling continues to build, using one of your hands, slightly pinch your thumbnail. Continue to pinch the thumbnail as the feeling builds.
- Keep on with this process until you have the most powerful feeling of fearlessness.
- Break state. You can stare at the ceiling or floor or use any other method you are comfortable with. It is important to break the state as you do not want to swish back to the former image.

Once you have completed the anchoring process, the next thing to do is to test (fire) the anchor. By firing the anchor, you ascertain whether or not you have created a powerful anchor. To test the anchor you have built, pinch your thumbnail as you did during the anchoring procedure. Notice what happens to you. Do you have that strong feeling of fearlessness? If you do, then congratulations, you have just created a fearlessness anchor! However, if you do not get the fearlessness feeling, start, and complete the process again. Then test. Still, don't feel it? Try again. Keep trying until you develop a powerful anchor.

Now that we have understood what anchors are and how they can be applied to great effect let's continue on our journey to ridding ourselves of fear.

Technique #1: The three-step fast phobia cure (originally designed by Richard Bandler)

Step 1: Look for a safe environment to reach out to fear.

- Create an image of a movie cinema. Do not be afraid to make full use of your imaginative prowess.
- Move into the cinema and locate the most comfortable, VIP seat available. Sit comfortably in it.
- Create a video of the fear you wish to overcome. This could be a short clip of a reaction you once had or a possible reaction to the fear, or the result of exposing yourself to it. Make sure the video is colored.
- Now, separate into two, keeping your original form and physique. This is called the *double dissociated state*. Keep a version of yourself seated and float the other version of yourself to the gallery where you can perch and watch both the version of yourself watching the screen and the screen itself.
- As you are watching a seated version of yourself as well as the screen, play the video you have created.
- Freeze the last frame of the video and change it from colored to grey.

Step 2: Associating the fear with healthy emotions.

- Think of your favorite song, one that makes you feel great. Connect the last (now grey) frame of your video to this song.
- Now play the video backward at a very fast rate (double the normal rate, or faster). When you get to the first frame, freeze it and turn it to grey.
- You may repeat step 2 in order to make it as smooth as possible.

Step 3: Dissociate yourself from the fear.

- Now float back from the gallery and rejoin the version of you sitting in the most comfortable seat in the cinema.
- Whiten out the screen.

- When you are ready, watch the video of your fear associated with your favorite music from start to finish in color. Notice your new reaction to the fear.
- If you don't have the desired feeling, repeat the procedure from start to finish.

Technique #2: Overcoming fear with NLP hypnosis

Step 1: Establish rapport with yourself.

While establishing and maintaining rapport with your own self might sound ridiculous, it is a vital first step in this technique – and many other techniques – of overcoming inherent fear. You must be able to develop an interest in your thoughts and emotions and how one leads to the creation of the other. After all, thoughts and emotions are the structures that create our experience. You need to be patient with, and kind to yourself. Encourage yourself. If the methods for doing this do not jump right at you, then use a proven, commonly used technique: treat yourself the way you treat the person you love and care about the most.

Step 2: Reframe your state of mind.

Change the way you visualize a problem by assessing the intentions behind your actions and behaviors that led to the problem. A problem might be a result of inappropriate handling of techniques or methods to accomplish an intention. In this sense, your actions and behaviors are not bad; they were just used poorly. Most fears harbored by individuals come from an episode or two of injudicious use of resources, the poor outcomes of which prevent the individuals from venturing into any further endeavor in that line of action. By changing the way you think and feel about bad outcomes, you can be more open to carrying out actions and less fearful of what the results might be, while making better use of your resources.

Step 3: Trigger the fear reaction.

The motive behind triggering the fear reaction is to allow yourself to identify and assess the signs of your response to the fear stimulus. While in this state, ask yourself pertinent questions such as, "What makes me fear? What if that thing presents itself here this moment?" Immediately you find yourself responding to these thoughts in a fearful manner (similar to how you usually respond to them), break state.

Step 4: Use the double dissociated state technique.

Go over the fourth point in step 1 of technique #1 to put yourself in a double dissociated state.

Step 5: Making a movie of your fear.

- Think of a time when you first had the fear, or when you felt it the most…or the most recent episode. Create a movie of it in black and white and watch it on the screen. Make sure to include sound in the movie and play it at a normal speed or frame rate.
- Watch yourself in the movie, and while so doing, continuously remind yourself that you are safe presently and that the fear cannot get you where you are at the moment. Then watch your other self in the theatre also watching the movie. Emphasize that it is just a movie.
- On reaching the end of the movie, freeze the last frame.

Step 6: Reunite with yourself.

Float away from the gallery and into your former self in the frozen frame on the screen. Then, play the movie backward from the end to the beginning, colored, at a very fast rate.

Step 7: Carry out a test.

Upon completion of the reverse running of the movie, test your responses by asking yourself questions that would have elicited the feeling of fear in you. The questions could be, "What makes me fear? What if that thing presents itself here this moment?" If you still feel fear, then run through the procedure again. Repeat the process as many times as it would be necessary to bring about the desired outcome.

Step 8: Perform an ecology check.

This is the stage where you evaluate your new responses to the fear triggers. What makes them different from the responses you used to exhibit? How can you ensure that you exhibit better responses in future circumstances?

Technique #3: Removing fear through visualization and anchoring

Step 1: Think about the fear.

The feeling generated by the fear should generally 'come' from a certain direction in your body. Identify this direction. Imagine that this fear is a physical thing, then move it out of your body, and put it back in such a way that it now wobbles in the opposite direction. Make the fear continue to wobble faster and faster, and while doing so, continuously think of the fear.

Step 2: Get to the root of the fear.

You need to find out the reason behind the fear. Certain fears, for example, help prepare an individual for defense or have protective functions. Find out positive ways you can achieve the reason or intention behind the fear, without resorting to the negative emotion of fear. This can prove invaluable if done correctly.

Step 3: Create powerful, fearless states, anchor them, and fire the anchors whenever you feel fear.

Step 4. Get aware of your physiology.

You may exhibit certain behaviors when afraid, such as assuming a certain posture or breathing in a certain way. Try adjusting your physiology, like adopting a new posture, breathing differently, or raising your shoulders.

Step 5: Lessen the weight of the fear.

Lighten your fear. A good way to do this is by making jokes about having the fear and literally laughing at your own jokes. This makes them fearless of a burden and easier to overcome. Do this routine and effectively enough, and you find yourself laughing at the thought of the fear.

Gaining Confidence

Lack of self-confidence is one of the foremost reasons why some entrepreneurs fail in business. Low confidence – in one's abilities, skills, ideas, and solutions – is also a major reason why some would-be entrepreneurs give up their dream to focus on other less weighty options such as focusing on a nine-to-five job. Confidence in oneself is a vital – and perhaps the most important – ingredient in the making of a successful entrepreneur. Without it, very little can be achieved no matter the weight of the opening balance in the checking account.

Confidence in yourself allows you to be able to make the best decisions and impact the workplace more positively. It also increases your satisfaction with yourself and your enterprise. You're the leader at the workplace, and, therefore, by staying confident and calm even in the face of adversity, you subtly urge your team to do the same. However, overconfidence has its own negatives. Having the confidence in your abilities to carry out tasks is one thing, having the actual abilities to perform is another, and as a leader, you should be able to discern between the two. As much as you believe in yourself, be in touch with yourself to know your limitations and when you need to call for help.

Low confidence in yourself prevents you from expressing your true abilities, no matter how good they are. Not being able to express your abilities means you cannot achieve success, and if you do, it would only be a shadow of what it could have been. Lack of success leads to a further decrease in self-confidence; it is a vicious cycle that destroys you and your business from within. Here are some other common effects of low self-confidence:

- Low self-confidence hinders spontaneity. It prevents you from acting when you really need to, because you do not think you have the ability to act or that your action would be praiseworthy. What's worse is, a person with low self-confidence may begin to interpret their low confidence as laziness or passiveness. This mindset severely hurts their potential to succeed.
- It makes you unwilling to test the waters. No amount of knowledge, expertise, or experience will make you try daring and active if your self-confidence is low.
- It affects your ability to create or maintain healthy relationships. When you have low confidence, you perpetually try to impress the people you are relating with, as you don't feel adequate or worthy enough to be in the relationship. Low confidence also increases your sensitivity, such that you get annoyed or hurt easily by people you are in a relationship with, causing unnecessary conflicts and fallouts.
- Low confidence deprives you of the enjoyment of celebrating your victories and achievements because you do not believe you have done enough to deserve the accomplishments.

- Either low self-confidence breeds perfectionism or perfectionism breeds low self-confidence. Whatever the case, there seems to be a strong correlation between the two, and as perfectionism is as unachievable as it is unreasonable, individuals suffering from low confidence are likely to get stuck rather than progressing and excelling. Lack of confidence also restrains you from seeking the help of others, as you feel asking for help dishonors your own self-respect.
- It also comes with a certain lack of motivation to act. If you don't believe in your own abilities to succeed, then what is the need to even try?
- On a personal level, individuals with low self-confidence tend to have a poor image of themselves, even if there is absolutely nothing wrong with their appearance.
- Low confidence people are usually passive or aggressive rather than assertive. Assertiveness is one of the best qualities of an entrepreneur, as it expresses confidence and calmness. Passiveness and aggressiveness in the business environment only elicit damaging negative responses.

NLP Techniques for Building Self-confidence

Low self-confidence, as we have seen from the points above, is a crucial attribute of successful individuals and a damning scourge of unsuccessful ones. No amount of work can make you as successful as you could possibly be if you lack the confidence to showcase your abilities and value. You need to be confident to command higher prices on your products and services, to demand and secure higher productivity and creativity from your staff, and to assert your authority at the workplace.

Lack of confidence simply derides your efforts and hampers your progress. Hence there is a need to develop your confidence level if it is low. Far from the popular belief that you are either born with self-confidence or lack it for the rest of your life, self-confidence is something you could actually develop. It can be nurtured consciously or unconsciously at any age and in almost any circumstances. Fortunately, there are many NLP Techniques that can help increase your level of confidence so you can always perform at turbo speed and machine efficiency.

Before getting started on the techniques to increase your confidence level, make a comprehensive list of all the times in the future, you think you could be let down by your low confidence. This could be specific occasions, such as an interview or more general events such as meeting with people. Ensure not to rush the process; take your time and make this list as comprehensive as possible, as the results you would get depend on its accuracy. You could also return to this list at any point in the process to alter or modify it as appropriate.

Once you have made your list, use the NLP swish technique to change the negative image of each of the items on the list to a more positive image. Let's quickly run through the swish technique again, in case you might have forgotten how to use it.

NLP Swish Technique

1. Ascertain the trigger(s) for the behavior. For example, you think you would lack the confidence to be successful at an interview because you feel the interviewers might have a problem with your tie. In this case, your tie is the trigger.

2. Develop a mental image of this trigger in your mind.

3. Identify the vital submodalities in that mental picture. For example, think about what makes the picture less attractive. Try reducing the brightness, changing it from color to black & white, changing its size or shape, or making it more distant.

4. Create a mental image of yourself without this undesired behavior. What would you look like without your poor confi-

dence level? Would you look and feel better? Create a vivid picture of a confident version of yourself. Ensure to spend quality time in this stage to get a strong mental picture, as the success of this technique depends on it.

5. Identify the vital submodalities in this desirable mental picture of yourself. Make it more attractive by tweaking certain submodalities. Try bringing it nearer, making the colors more vivid and bright, increasing the size of the image, or adding background music.

6. Check if you agree with this desirable mental picture. Do you have any worries concerning how this desirable image might affect your life?

7. Now, bring the two mental images you now have side by side, or make them overlap, whichever works for you, but make the undesired image large, colorful, and attractive while leaving the desired image small, bland, and unattractive.

8. Quickly explode the desired image into a large, attractive image and simultaneously shrink the undesired image into a small, distasteful picture while making a swiiiiissssshhhh sound. Allow this new image to linger for a few seconds to savor its attractiveness.

9. Break state. You can stare at the ceiling or floor or use any other method you are comfortable with. It is important to break the state as you do not want to swish back to the former image.

10. Quickly repeat steps 5 to 9 at least four times.

11. Test. See if thinking about the undesirable image brings the desirable image to mind immediately.

12. Do this for the remaining items on your list.

Apart from the swish technique, there are other NLP techniques that you can employ to bolster your self-confidence successfully. These techniques include the *NLP Get Grounded* exercise, the *Mommy, Make it Go Away* technique, the *NLP Whiteout* technique, the NLP technique to kill nagging voices, and *NLP Anchoring* technique.

We'll now dive headfirst into each of these techniques. As always, it is highly recommended that you try out all of these techniques and then make a habit of performing the ones that work for you best.

NLP Get Grounded Exercise for Boosting Confidence

This exercise is a brief one that has been used in many NLP inspired workshops and lectures to help people increase their self-confidence. It is also exceedingly useful in preparation for social functions or interviews. It goes as thus:

1. Remove your shoes. While this is not exactly mandatory for the success of the exercise, it is recommended that you keep your feet flat on the ground or floor. If you are in an office, however, you may keep your shoes on. It is not recommended to wear high heels for this exercise as your feet must be as flat as possible.
2. Stand on your feet. The NLP grounding exercise is not one of those techniques that require the practitioner to sit and imagine. You need to be on your feet for this exercise to come through. If you have a problem standing (if you are in a wheelchair, for example), you could sit straight with your feet touching the ground.
3. Point your feet in a forward direction and spread them apart to about the width of your shoulders.
4. Check that your feet are flat on the ground, then grip the ground with your toes.
5. With your toes now gripping the ground, gently rotate your hips inwardly a bit. This might feel a little uncomfortable, but it would all be worth it in the end.
6. Ensure that your shoulders are relaxed and arms are in a loose position.
7. Slightly relax your knees.

8. Keep your legs in an upright position, but do not lock your knees.
9. Breathe out and slightly sink your body.
10. Locate a point about 2 inches below your navel and focus your attention on it. If the positioning is correct, this point should be where you feel the tenseness in your stomach muscles. You should also feel as though this point is the center of your balance and support.
11. While keeping your body in a relaxed state, take deep, slow breaths in and out continuously.
12. Make sure to spend plenty of time perfecting this position. Once the position becomes comfortable for you, make it a habit to get into it for some minutes every day. When you become very familiar with it, try moving whilst keeping your focus on the central point. It may be somewhat weird at first to move around in this position, but soon you would come to terms with it and feel more comfortable in it. Pay particular attention to your breathing as it could change without your notice.

Practice several times until getting into this position becomes very fluid and convenient. You should be able to maintain and walk around in this position in public in no distant time and retain the position even while still. This position gives people the impression that you are grounded, confident, and calm.

Mommy, Make it Go Away Technique

This NLP technique allows you to replace the negative feelings you have whenever you think of an uncomfortable event from your past with positive feelings. This could be an interview, a class presentation, a project defense, or any other experience. For this technique to be put to effective use, you must have a solid knowledge of NLP submodalities – which you do – and a good knowledge of the NLP memory manipulation technique – which you don't...yet. So, let's start with the memory manipulation technique, get grounded in it, and thereafter slide into the Mommy, make it go away technique.

The NLP memory manipulation technique is a technique used to alter memories of events or experiences. In NLP, it is presupposed that when we remember an event, we do so with our five senses – we remember what we saw, heard, felt, smelled, and tasted. Mostly, only three of these five senses (visual, auditory, and kinesthetic) are used for NLP purposes. So, in essence, by remembering an event, we are attempting to recollect what we saw, heard, and felt, but in a subjective manner. In this light, we create internal representations bypassing what actually happened through our internal filters, such as beliefs, education, and values. By manipulating these internal representations, we could always restructure our memories. There are several exercises you can take to alter the content of your memory. Let's get ourselves familiar with three of these exercises.

- Exercise 1
  - Imagine a person who ridicules you, someone who makes you feel unworthy or unimportant, someone who usually gets the better of you in an argument, or someone who belittles your contributions in a group discussion. Create an image of that person in your head.
  - Create an image of you dealing with that person sometime in the future.
  - Assess the image and find all of the unrealistic features therein. Turn all unrealistic characteristics of the image realistic. For example, if the person that bothers you is unreasonably tall in your mental picture, shrink them. If they are extraordinarily huge, making them slimmer. Do this for all the other unrealistic features.
  - Now, you are going to make some of the realistic features in the image unrealistic. For example, give their faces a huge clown's nose. Now observe how the person seems now. Is the person still scary or intimidating? How about giving them really big blue pants? How do they look now?

65

- Exercise 2
  - Imagine someone whose voice bothers you or has bothered you in the past, someone whose voice intimidates you or makes you uncomfortable.
  - Change their voice. If the person has a stern, commanding voice, what happens when you make them sound like Donald Duck, or when you increase their speech speed until they begin to sound like squabbling mice? You could use the help of a search engine if you have no idea what Donald Duck sounds like.
  - If the person has a really smooth speech, slow them down and make them talk incoherently.

- Exercise 3
  - Remember four or five people who give you a hard time.
  - Imagine the next time you would have to relate to them.
  - Use visual submodalities in your mind to make your encounter with them easier for yourself. For example, you could give them a big clown's nose, make their gait wobbly, give them a terrible haircut, make them wear a dress meant for the opposite sex, or give them features of the opposite sex (if the person is a woman, give her a mustache).
  - Use auditory submodalities in your mind to make your encounter with them easier for yourself. For example, you could make them sound like Donald Duck, make them speak slowly in a funny way, or make them sound like the opposite sex.
  - You could also use kinesthetic submodalities to make them easier to deal with. You could, for example, make yourself feel like laughing hysterically on thinking of them.

These exercises are very easy to use, and once mastered, you could use them to modify almost any memory you are struggling with. Let us now glide into the "Mommy, make it go away" technique proper. Here go the steps:

1. Think of the memory you want to let go. As you think of it, notice that the image of the memory has a definite location somewhere in your mind.
2. Ascertain the exact location of the image – in front of you, by your right, by your left, or behind you.
3. Take the image and move it nearer a bit and back to its original position. By now, you know you can change the position of the image.
4. Imagine that you have a huge catapult (or a slingshot) in front of you.
5. Imagine that the image is perched in the catapult.
6. With all of your strength, pull the elastic band of the catapult all the way back until it reaches its elastic limit. Then, let go.
7. Watch the image shoot off into the distance until it becomes a tiny speck in space.
8. Think about something entirely different.
9. Think of the memory you just catapulted into an abyss. Is the image still in the same position as it was earlier? If it still is, don't be afraid to give it another dose of catapulting. Repeat this step until the image becomes only a tiny speck in space whenever you think of it.

NLP Whiteout Technique

Similar to the Mommy, make it go away technique, the whiteout technique is a technique used to forget uncomfortable memories permanently. Bad memories can affect your present and challenge your ability to make progress. With the NLP whiteout technique, you can push those bugging memories out of your consciousness for good.

1. Think of something that makes you feel uncomfortable. It could be a memory of a time you embarrassed yourself at an interview or gave a terrible presentation.

2. Make the image as lucid as possible.
3. Increase the white balance of the image quickly until it turns completely white.
4. Break state. This step is important so that your brain does not create a loop.
5. Repeat steps 3 and 4 five more times.
6. Remember the memory and notice what happens. Notice that the image either whites out automatically or is completely white and you cannot see it clearly.
7. If you do not achieve the results you want, repeat the process all over again. In the repeat process, try performing the whiteout faster and adding sound effects.

NLP Technique to Kill Nagging Voices

This NLP technique can be used to destroy the voices of hesitancy in one's mind. It is potent in summoning courage and confidence to carry out a task, such as speaking in public or offering your solution at a workshop. The steps are simple and straightforward and are presented in the following lines.

1. Think of a time you wanted to do something, but a nagging voice told you not to.
2. Notice that the voice comes from a certain direction in your mind. Also, try to ascertain whose voice it is. Is it really your voice or that of someone else?
3. Know exactly what the voice sounds like.
4. Change the location of the voice, so that it now comes from a distant place in your mind, and you can only hear it faintly. Is there a change in the effect the voice has on you now?
5. Change some of the characteristics of the voice and see what happens. For example, you could change the voice to that of Donald Duck.
6. Add certain features to the voice to make it seem less important or serious. Try adding background music from one of Charlie Chaplin's films. How does the voice sound now?

7. Repeat the exercise if it doesn't work out at the first try. Do this for all the nagging voices in your head and send them out.

NLP Anchoring Technique to Gain Confidence

We have run through some anchoring techniques in previous sections of this book, so we should be decently familiar with NLP anchoring and anchors by now. Let's look at how you can build powerful anchors that you can use to boost your self-confidence.

1. Remember a time in the past when you had your highest confidence level. If there has not been such a time, then you could simply imagine it. Create a mental picture of you being super confident...the most confident you could possibly be.
2. Once you have that image in your mind, play around the auditory submodalities of the image. If the image has no sounds yet, add relevant sounds to strengthen the state. Notice how the image makes you feel now.
3. Once you have that image on your mind, add the appropriate visual and auditory submodalities to make it even more appealing. 'Appropriate' in this sense means the submodalities that make the image more attractive to you. Also, notice the way you feel about the image. What you are doing is trying to achieve as strong a mental state as you can develop.
4. Keep the feeling building through your body by fixating the mental image to your mind.
5. As the feeling continues to build, using one of your hands, slightly pinch your thumbnail. Continue to pinch the thumbnail as the feeling builds. Note that you could build an anchor on any part of your body...it doesn't have to be your thumbnail all the time. You could use your toes or knuckles.

You also do not have to pinch…a tap, or a slight press can do the trick as well.

6. Keep on with this process until you have the most powerful feeling of confidence.

7. Break state by concentrating on something else.

8. Once you have completed the anchoring process, the next thing to do is test the anchor. By firing the anchor, you ascertain whether or not you have created a powerful anchor. To test the anchor you have built, pinch your thumbnail as you did during the anchoring procedure. Notice what happens to you. Do you have that strong feeling of confidence? If you do, then congratulations, you have just created a confidence anchor! However, if you do not get the feeling of confidence you are looking for, start, and complete the process again. Then test. Still, don't feel it? Try again. Keep trying until you develop a powerful anchor.

All of these techniques are effective in quickly boosting your self-confidence. You may choose to use any one of them or use a combination of two or more; the choice is yours really. One thing to keep in mind is that every technique must be practiced adequately and mastered for effective use. While you are unto mastering these techniques to boost your confidence, you may as well work along with the following guidelines and self-help rules for optimization of the confidence-boosting process.

- Your self-talk affects you.

How do you talk to yourself? Do you engage in conversations with yourself in a respectful and courteous manner, or do you self-hate and self-criticize? You are worthy of all the respect you give to other people. Give some of that respect to yourself when you self-talk. Talking negatively or contemptuously can have a huge negative impact on your life, your relationships, and your business. You can build your confidence from within by consciously talking to yourself in a positive, empowering, loving manner. If you would be anywhere near business success, you must learn the art of positive self-talk. After all, if you don't love and believe in yourself, who will?

- Act it before you feel it

In business, time is of the essence. You need to stop waiting to feel strongly confident and start behaving and performing as though you already are. No matter how many times you practice the NLP techniques detailed out in this book, if you do not start acting confidently immediately, you may never really feel as confident as you would like. Acting confident rewires your brain to visualize and respond to experiences in a better, more positive manner. When your brain does this, you get clearer internal representations of what you see, hear, and feel, and respond to them more positively. Hence, your confidence grows.

- Vivify your purpose

If you feel unsure about your purpose, then you might struggle to achieve success. Having a defined vision is the fuel that drives you to perform. If you lack a defined "why" on a task, you are going to lack the motivation required to thrive at the task. Hence, you resort to self-doubt. You must have a clear, concise purpose of creating and developing a business venture, aside from making profits. Apart from making your entrepreneurial journey a lot less bumpy, a clear purpose helps you set better goals and aligns you with better pathways to achieve your goals. Furthermore, as you achieve success at a business that has a defined purpose, you not only accrue more profits but also feel more satisfied with yourself and your actions. This helps boost self-confidence.

- Get rid of your fear of failing

The popular misconception that entrepreneurs are totally devoid of fear cannot be further from the truth. We all have fears. Everyone does, including the most successful entrepreneurs. However, the difference between successful and unsuccessful entrepreneurs is that the successful ones have chosen to act regardless of their fears and phobias. Learn not to take failures as woes or hardships, but as opportunities to learn and develop.

- Exercise the confidence muscle

Just like a muscle that gets built through regular exercise, confidence builds through constant practice. The more you practice being confident, the stronger your feeling of confidence gets. Nobody was born with a confidence ring hanging around their neck; confidence is developed through conscious (and unconscious) actions and behaviors. Rid your life of habits, thoughts, behaviors, and emotions that deteriorate your self-image and self-confidence and imbibe those that exacerbate them. Practice being confident consciously until you begin to act confident unconsciously. In other words, "fake it till you feel it."

CHAPTER 4: SELF-APPRECIATION AND SELF-ESTEEM

Self-Appreciation

Self-appreciation is the opposite of self-blame. It is saying thank you to yourself for all of your efforts. Self-appreciation is about being grateful for who you are, what you are, and what resources you have – including your physical, intellectual, emotional, and social attributes. In a world that is rooted in high self-esteem, we tend to be forced to express ourselves as being better than average.

Hence, we focus on the outward and neglect the inward attributes of our being. We constantly see ourselves through the eyes of other people and judge our abilities and attributes from their perspective. Hence, our valuation of ourselves is perpetually contingent on the judgments of others. The basis of self-appreciation lies in the reverse direction – to see ourselves for who we truly are and be grateful for how we are.

Self-appreciation must not be confused for self-pity or self-indulgence; it does not mean being self-centered. When people indulge in self-pity, they tend to focus on themselves and immerse themselves in the thought that they are always on the receiving end and are suffering more than any other person in the world. By pitying yourself, you are perpetually playing victim, and as you do so, you slowly but surely lose control over yourself and your fate. Self-indulgence, on the other hand, is a way to escape reality – to focus on other than the matters that are pertinent to your life and success.

Self-appreciation is about caring for what you have, getting in tune with yourself, and having a healthy relationship with yourself. It is valuing what you have and making the best use of the resources available to you in a positive, optimistic manner. As Malcolm Forbes says, "Too many people overvalue what they are not and undervalue what they are." This statement is true to the extent that people seem to value external appreciation in an exaggerated way and use whatever appreciation they get from other people as a means of measuring their own worth and value.

You do not have to become someone or something else to appreciate yourself; you must appreciate what you already have and who you already are. However, self-appreciation does not promote self-limiting, as it is not meant to encourage you to remain the same and never progressing. You could appreciate who you already are whilst still engaging in behaviors that are aimed at making you a better person, as long as you are striving to be a better person for you, and not because you feel under pressure to be someone else. Self-appreciation is being fully aware of your strengths and weaknesses, your abilities and flaws, your beauty and faults, and appreciating yourself all the same. It is loving who you are even though you are not perfect, without pretending that you are something you are not.

When we begin to look inward for appreciation, we tend to find negatives rather than the positive things about ourselves. This bias in our thinking is at the root of the discontent in society and the main reason why we continually strive for improvement and even perfection. A way to get out of this rat race of needless self-criticism is to practice self-appreciation consciously. If self-appreciation does not come easy to you, you could take the following steps to help you out.

- Think of something you appreciate about yourself — just one thing. You could be a funny, smart, intelligent, or a good leader.
- Think of one time when you noticed this quality about yourself. Notice how good feelings well up in you.

- Verbally acknowledge this quality in you by saying, "I am *so*." For example, "I am smart." Say this repeatedly at various speeds and different volumes.
- Savor the feeling by saying each statement for as long as ten seconds and in the best way you can.
- As you repeat the statement continuously, the feeling of self-appreciate eventually begins to slip away. Bring your focus back to the statement and arouse that feeling of appreciation again.

Notice how you feel about yourself now that you appreciate yourself more. The aim of this exercise is to rewire your brain to focus on the positives and shift attention from the negatives in yourself. Self-appreciation should not make you supercilious or narcissistic, but rather stronger and more resilient to the inevitable external forces that sometimes trigger us to focus on our negative ends. A major scourge of self-appreciation is comparison. Society, particularly in this age, has turned us into competitors, making us compare and contrast between ours and other people's skills and abilities. It is hard to love and appreciate yourself in these circumstances. However, a constant reminder to ourselves that we are neither perfect nor meant to be, and that we are unique and wonderful just the way we are can go a long way in eliciting a feeling of appreciation in ourselves.

Self-Esteem

Self-esteem is commonly defined as a person's subjection estimation of their worth or value. It is an individual's personal statement about their belief in their own worth – in simple terms, how much they love themselves. Self-esteem is one of the most commonly discussed psychosocial matters in general, as it is believed to be the underlying factor behind and a major determinant of certain outcomes, such as academic or entrepreneurial accomplishments, happiness, and criminality. In essence, it can be stated that a good level of self-esteem is a belief in oneself and one's self-worth and low self-esteem teeters on disbelief in oneself.

According to research, 85 percent of the world's population suffers from a variety of low self-esteem. That's quite a high number! It means eight to nine out of every ten persons in the world suffer this scourge. Additionally, it is proven that the victims of low self-esteem are not only uneducated or poor people of society but also some of the more learned and wealthy individuals in the world.

A normal level of self-esteem is a must-have trait for true success. Notice the use of 'normal' rather than the word 'high.' High self-esteem, like low self-esteem, has its own flaws. While low self-esteem cripples your mind and leaves you feeling depressed, too high self-esteem can have serious psychosocial effects on you – one of which is the well-known narcissistic personality disorder – and hurt your relationships. Therefore, it is best to aim at balanced self-esteem, which is neither at the extremely high nor extremely low end of the spectrum.

The entrepreneurial world is one that is constantly demanding and evolving, and as such one that requires that entrepreneurs continually show their flexibility and creativity in presenting solutions. Entrepreneurs who are more confident in themselves and their products tend to thrive in this highly competitive world, leaving those who have little faith in themselves and their products on the fringes. Belief in oneself emanates from having a decent sense of self-worth, believing that one has the right to *be*.

While self-confidence and self-esteem have been used interchangeably over time, it is worthy of note to state that they are two distinct phenomena. Self-esteem is how much you value yourself or your opinion and would often apply to all facets of your life. On the other hand, self-confidence is your belief in your abilities and applies to certain situations.

For example, an individual with good self-esteem may have low confidence in situations that involve dancing. This does not mean they have low self-esteem in general, but that particular situation is one they do not believe they have the requisite abilities to excel in. In general, a person with low self-esteem would have some or all of the following traits:

- They are very critical of themselves
- They often undervalue their positives and overvalue their negatives
- They think other people are better than them
- They tend to use negative words while talking about or describing themselves
- They blame themselves for the faults of others and are not quick to accept praise or take credit for what they have done well
- They have a hard time believing genuinely positive things people say about them

If you notice that you have exhibited any of these behaviors sometime in the past or are still doing so now, then your self-esteem level may need working on. If you do not develop your self-esteem to a good level, some of the effects your low self-esteem would have on you are:

- You may find yourself always dissatisfied about the way you are, and as a result, feel depressed, anxious, sad, or guilty.
- You may have relationship problems, as you find it difficult to express in clear terms what you want from a relationship. You could endure certain things you wouldn't have if your self-esteem were not low.
- Because of your low self-worth, you avoid trying to accomplish anything or shy away from actions that could put you in situations where you would have to relate with other people.
- You could aim for perfection as you continuously push yourself to over-achieve as atonement for lacking self-esteem.
- When you have low self-esteem, you care very little about your health and wellbeing. Hence, you may indulge in be-

haviors that can put your life at risk, such as excessive alcohol intake.

- Low self-esteem has been identified as a major factor contributing to the disparities in the income of entrepreneurs undertaking the same or similar business ventures.
- If you are considering starting your own business or have a business idea you wish to inculcate into your current enterprise, low self-esteem might prevent you from pursuing the idea, and instead encourage you to stay put in your comfort zone. People with good self-esteem are much more likely to pursue a business idea that people who have low self-esteem.
- People with low self-esteem are not risk-takers. As a result, they are slow in progressing business-wise.

Needless to say, low self-esteem is an enterprise killer and a dream crusher. If you are unfortunately caught up in its grasp, don't fret, NLP has got you covered. Just as it does for self-confidence, NLP has several techniques that are designed to raise your self-esteem to a level you can be happy about. There are many NLP techniques that have been designed to help give you a self-esteem boost. They include the ten-step self-esteem enhancer, the seven-step self-esteem booster, the six-step reframing technique, the NLP belief creator technique, and the NLP belief disintegrator technique. We will now look into these techniques one after another.

NLP Ten-Step Self-Esteem Enhancer

The ten-step self-esteem enhancer is a 10-step exercise founded on NLP principles and developed to create positive feelings within you that can help you ride smoothly through the day. It is best utilized up your *ante* when your self-esteem and self-confidence levels are low. It is recommended that you run this exercise on a daily schedule – for example, you could run through it twice a day in the morning before work and at night before bed. You could also practice it at any point during the day that you feel low in self-esteem or self-

78

confidence. One thing to remember as you perform this exercise is that it is not a magic wand that can recharge your self-esteem instantly; instead, it is a tool that only gets better through constant use. Let us now run through the exercise.

1. Relax your body, close your eyes, and take deep breaths in and out. Think of a person who you know truly cares about you. Create a mental picture of this person and focus on what makes them beautiful to look at.

2. Imagine that you are sitting behind a desk. With a beautifully designed pen and a finely crafted hardcover book, begin to write your autobiography. Write out all of your experiences from the day you discovered you're being to the present day and the possible future. As you are writing, imagine that that person that loves you is standing close, separated from you by a glass barrier, and watching you as you write.

3. As you picture this person, start to write about them in your autobiography. Write down all their good features and qualities, as well as all of the experiences you have shared with them. Notice how you feel about this person in general, about their presence in your life, and about the fact that they genuinely love you.

4. As you continue to write and feel, this person is now smiling at you from behind the glass barrier. Their smile is radiant and true, and it leaves you feeling good. Now, dissociate into two. With a part of you still seated at the desk, float the other part to where this person is standing and stand next to them. Now both of you are watching the other version of you that is still writing your autobiography.

5. Look at how beautifully you are seated behind the desk and how well you are writing. Notice how you see yourself from this perspective. Ask yourself, "What do I like about this person I'm watching? What am I capable of doing? What abilities do I possess?"

6. Now step inside the loving person you have been standing next to and begin to see through their eyes. Try to see as they

would see, hear as they would hear, and feel as they would feel about you. You and this person are now one. You are now this person who truly loves and adores you.

7. As you see, hear, and feel from this loving person's perspective, ask yourself, "What does this loving, wonderful person think of me? How do they feel about me? What do they think I'm capable of doing?" As you continue to ponder over these questions, try as much as you can not to utter the first answers that come to you; take them as they come.

8. Slowly detach yourself from this person, and as you do so, keep the answers you just got from the questions you asked earlier. Keep them with you, as if they are your own views. Now transfer these feelings to the "you" behind the desk who is still writing. On doing so, so, write about the feelings you now have about yourself in your autobiography. Write about how your new views about yourself are different from the old views you used to have.

9. At this point, begin to write about your future in a positive light. Write about how the feelings you now have about yourself have changed your life for the better. Answer questions such as, "How do I feel about myself now? How has my future changed with the emergence of these new feelings? How much more self-esteem and self-confidence do I now possess? What challenges am I now willing to undertake? What are the positives in this new me that can make me succeed at whatever I want to do?" Make sure to provide an adequate answer to each question proceeding to the next. Commit to inculcating these new feelings you have about yourself into everything you do.

10. Finish writing your autobiography, and as you round up, imagine that the lights in the room have begun to dim slowly. As the lights slowly go out, gradually return to the present reality. Feel the new positive energy that now runs through your entire body as you now love and value yourself more.

Self-esteem is quite simply a necessity you cannot do without if your aim is business and professional success. It is the foundation upon which you must base your efforts and attempts to create something different. If for any reason this foundation is weak, then you need to deal with the rot with the NLP techniques I have highlighted above. It is important that you fix any underlying fear and esteem issues before you can approach success with assured steps.

NLP Seven-Step Self-Esteem Booster

Another vital NLP technique routinely used to improve self-esteem is the NLP seven-step self-esteem booster. This technique is useful when you need a boost in self-esteem and self-confidence either to carry out a task or simply to feel good about yourself. You could also use this technique to heal from past experiences that have dealt with your self-esteem a significant blow. Quite literally, the seven-step self-esteem booster is a dose of self-esteem to use whenever you need it. So let's get to it. Try out the following steps to give yourself a surge in self-esteem:

1. Be in the know of your state of mind throughout the day. This is the first step in the process. You must ensure to stay vigilant of how you feel about yourself in every moment of the day. Whenever you become aware that you are getting low on self-esteem or lacking in self-confidence, give yourself a break from whatever it is you are doing and run through the rest of this exercise.
2. Carry out a self-evaluation. When you find out that you are not feeling your best, you would need to carry out a self-assessment to ascertain your exact state of mind. To do this, ask yourself these questions:
- What is the specific problem I'm facing right now?
- How do I feel about this problem?
- Why do I feel the way I do about this problem?

- What is my internal focusing mechanism like? How is my mind focusing on things?
- How am I reacting to things externally?
- Why do I react to things this way?
- How do I self-talk? Am I talking to myself the appropriate way?
- What is my tone of voice like when I'm talking to myself?
- In what ways am I moving my body?
- Why do I move my body in this manner?
- How is my breathing and body posture?
- What are my beliefs about myself?
- How is my mind interpreting the challenges I'm experiencing?
- What assertions about my challenging am I making?
- Have I discovered a new thing about myself that I didn't know before now?
- What factors are preventing me from feeling good in these circumstances?

The goal of this self-assessment is to find out the factors that are stopping you from feeling good in this particular situation. By answering these questions, you gain clarity about why you are presently not feeling your best. Some of these questions require significant reasoning to get answered, so, endeavor to put in the mental work to answer them as objectively and prudently as you can. The more accurately and clearly you can answer these questions, the more confidence you will have that you can get up on top of your present situation.

3. Create a mental picture of a future version of you basking in a good level of self-esteem. This version of you should feel very confident, strong-minded, and capable of handling any task. This future version of you should be able to take care of your present situation with ease. Make sure this future you are not in the distant future but in the near future.

4. Evaluate your future self. Visualize and assess how your future self is handling things and how their methods of taking

care of situations are different from yours. Pay special attention to the confidence with which they're handlings things, and evaluate how they are able to run their affairs so smoothly by asking these questions:

- How is my future self-feeling?
- Why do they feel this way?
- How does their mind focus on things internally?
- How does their mind focus on things externally?
- Why do they focus on things the way they do?
- What tone of voice do they use while engaging in self-talk?
- What are the exact words they use?
- What are their beliefs about themselves?
- How do they move?
- How is their breathing and body posture?
- How do they interpret the events happening around them?
- What does your future self think of their 'present' circumstances?
- How are they relating to other people?
- Are they in a good mood and at peace with themselves?
- How have they attained this level of excitement and happiness? What are the things they had to do to get to this state?

The purpose of these questions is to find out the resources and behaviors that are necessary to attain the level of self-esteem and confidence you need at present. The answer to these questions should challenge you to find the intellectual and emotional understanding of what it takes to get the level of self-esteem you want.

5. Create a picture of your present self (who has low self-esteem) side-by-side with your future self (who is brimming with self-esteem and confidence). Make the picture as clear as possible, and a true representation of both your present situation and your future expectation. Assess the picture and pick out the telling differences between your present and future self. Now separate the picture into two – your present self and future self. Insert the picture of your present self in a

glass bubble and that of your future self in an identical glass bubble.

6. Reach for the glass bubble containing the image of your future self and shrink it. Shrink it more and more, until it becomes the size of a bean. Then, make it larger and larger until it reaches your own body size. Continue to shrink and expand the image and as you do that, feel the self-esteem and confidence of your future self crawl through your body and change your present emotional reality. While you are at this, say these to yourself:

- I am feeling good about myself.
- I have confidence in myself and my abilities.
- I am empowered to deal with any challenge that stands in my way.

Now, reach for the glass bubble containing the image of your present self and put it in front of that containing your future self. Then, take the glass bubble containing the picture of your present self and make it bigger and bigger until it reaches life-size. Now, poke a hole in the bubble and watch it deflate. As this bubble deflates and shrinks, watch the glass bubble of your future self come to the forefront and overshadow that of your present self completely. Feel the positive energy that rushes through your body as you continue to do this, and watch it transform your present situation. Again, affirm these statements to yourself:

- I am feeling good about myself.
- I have confidence in myself and my abilities.
- I am empowered to deal with any challenge that stands in my way.

7. Clone the glass bubble containing the image of your future self to produce many identical glass bubbles. Now, stack them on top of one another. Then, pick up the glass bubbles and insert them into your timeline, past and present. Now you have succeeded in populating your past and present with positive emotions. As you wake up every day of your life,

you simply absorb the positive energy you have placed already in it. This should give you the self-esteem you need to get through any day.

The Six-Step Reframing Technique

A third NLP technique we're going to look into and apply to boost our self-esteem is the six-step reframing technique. The six-step reframing technique is used to bring about behavioral change. It can be used to kill bad behavior or habit and replace it with a better one. The concept of reframing is based on the notion that our mind, just like our body, is divided into different parts. These parts of the mind are responsible for the actions we take. So, with reframing, you can train a part of the mind responsible for a bad action, behavior, or habit to start acting in a certain way. Individuals with low self-esteem have a bad habit of downplaying their abilities and exaggerating their flaws. Reframing can be used to replace this undesirable habit with a positive one. The six steps of NLP reframing are as follows:

Step 1: Identify what you want to change

As a first step, you must identify clearly the behavior, attitude, habit, or response you find undesirable and which you want to change. For example, you may want to change the negative manner in which you treat yourself.

Step 2: Communicate with the troubling part

Try to establish communication with the part of your mind responsible for the troubling behavior or response. Ask the part if it would like to engage in a conscious discussion with you. Note that this communication may be a picture, a voice, or a feeling in your mind. If you do receive a response from the part, thank it for responding. It is important to appreciate a response from the part, as it may already feel bad for having been alienated by you.

Step 3: Ascertain the positive intention

One of the basic presuppositions of NLP is that behind every behavior lies a positive intention. You must find the positive intention-behavior behind this undesirable behavior of yours. Ask the part, "What is it that you want? What is the positive intention behind this behavior you are exhibiting?" The purpose of these questions is to discern between the behavior, the intention behind it, and the way your mind is going about fulfilling the intention.

It is possible, even as humans, for our good intentions to get mis-construed by a person we are trying to help. They might even get angry at us because they interpreted our actions wrongly. In such situations as this, we may not be willing to render assistance to that person a second time. This is similar to how our unconscious mind works. It is sincerely doing its best to fulfill positive intentions for our own good, but sometimes we misinterpret what it is attempting to do, and even get angry at it for its responses. Just as you cannot be motivated to wake up early by someone who constantly tells you what a lazy person you are for waking up so late, you cannot change an undesirable behavior by shaming your mind. You need to build rapport with your mind to motivate it to change

Step 4: Create other ways

Once you know the positive intention behind your bad behavior, ask the creative part of your mind to create 3 other ways to go about fulfilling the intention.

Step 5: Evaluate the alternatives

Ask the part to assess the alternative options to see if it agrees with them. Find out whether these other ways of fulfilling the positive intention would be as good as or better than the one that created the undesirable behavior in the first place. The part must be willing to try out these new alternative pathways. Do not attempt to push the troubling part into accepting and trying these new options out. You must instead negotiate with it so that it willingly accepts to give them a go. If you find that the part does not approve of the new options, go back to step 4 and create new alternatives.

Step 6: Carry out an ecology check

Once you have successfully convinced the part to try out new alternatives to fulfilling an intention, carry out an ecology check to determine if the new behavior we are trying to adopt will be beneficial to us and the people around us. If your new behavior is thinking positively about yourself and your abilities, check to ensure that it does not, for example, make you start to feel or act over-confident or arrogant. If an ecology check comes out negative for a certain behavior, go back to step 2 and complete the entire reframing process from there.

NLP Belief Disintegrator Technique

This technique is used to destroy or annul negative or limiting beliefs, such as a belief that you don't have what it takes to lead. You may also start this exercise with a minor belief before moving on to a major one. The steps in this process are as follows:

1. Think of a thing you truly don't believe. You don't need to think of anything extraordinary; think of something simple, such as the belief that air is blue. As you think of this belief, notice that there is something related to it. For example, you can tell that the mental image of this belief is located somewhere in space. Is it located to the left or right? How far away is it positioned? Are there sounds attached to the image of this belief? When you have ascertained the position of this image, label it 'position A'. Now break state – think of something different, such as the last time it rained.

2. Now think of a thing you have no idea whether it is true or false, something you may not really care about at all. For example, think of whether the egg came before the chicken or the chicken came before the egg or any other thing you are

87

unsure about. As you think of this, notice that there is something attached to this thought as well. Where in space is the thought located? Is it located to the left or right? How far away is it positioned? When you have ascertained the position of this image, label it 'position B'.

3. Now you have two positions in your mind. Think of the new belief you want to generate and note where its image is positioned. Now move this image first to position B, and then to position A. You may experience certain problems in this step. Some of these are:

   a. The image may not move from one side to the other, for example, from right to left. You can solve this problem in three steps:

      i. Move the image from where it is – left side, for example – to the center.

      ii. Move it far away into the distance until it almost vanishes.

      iii. Move it towards yourself and slide it onto the other side – right side, for example.

   b. The image may go back to its original position. You can solve this by:

      i. Nailing the image in place

      ii. Locking it in place

      iii. Swishing (swiiiiiishhhhh) to secure it in the position of your choice

4. When the image is finally in the appropriate position, make sure it has the same size as the original image. Break state – think of something different. Think of the belief you just created. How does it feel now? Is it still in position A? Does your mind tell you that the belief is true? If the answers to these questions are negative, go back and retake the steps. Once you have successfully destroyed a negative belief, you can then use the NLP belief creator technique to create a new, positive belief.

NLP Belief Creator Technique

The belief creator technique is the direct opposite of the belief disintegrator technique. If you are struggling with self-doubt and low self-esteem, the NLP belief creator can help you generate new beliefs about yourself so you can feel your best always. For example, you can create a belief that you have the ability to lead. Even if it isn't true, it is still better to hold on to this belief that the opposite belief. Before you start out on creating a new belief, you must erase any trace of doubt from your mind, to maximize the outcome of this exercise. It is recommended that you attempt this exercise several times with a minor belief before trying with a major, life-changing belief. Here are the steps to create a brand-new belief:

1) Think of a thing you truly believe. You don't need to think of anything extraordinary; a simple belief that you can breathe, eat, or sleep will do. As you think of this belief, notice that there is something related to it. For example, you can tell that the mental image of this belief is located somewhere in space. Is it located to the left or right? How far away is it positioned? Are there sounds attached to the image of this belief? When you have ascertained the position of this image, label it 'position A'. Now break state – think of something different, such as the last time it rained.

2) Now think of a thing you have no idea whether it is true or false, something you may not really care about at all. For example, think of whether the egg came before the chicken or the chicken came before the egg or any other thing you are unsure about. As you think of this, notice that there is something attached to this thought as well. Where in space is the thought located? Is it located to the left or right? How far away is it positioned? When you have ascertained the position of this image, label it 'position B'.

3) Now you have two positions in your mind. Think of the new belief you want to generate and note where its image is positioned. Now move this image first to position B, and then to

position A. You may experience certain problems in this step. Some of these are:

- **a.** The image may not move from one side to the other, for example, from right to left. You can solve this problem in three steps:
    - i. Move the image from where it is – left side, for example – to the center.
    - ii. Move it far away into the distance until it almost vanishes.
    - iii. Move it towards yourself and slide it onto the other side – right side, for example.
- b. The image may go back to its original position. You can solve this by:
    - i. Nailing the image in place
    - ii. Locking it in place
    - iii. Swishing (swiiiiiiishhhhh) to secure it in the position of your choice

When the image is finally in the appropriate position, make sure it has the same size as the original image.

4) Break state – think of something different. Think of the belief you just created. How does it feel now? Is it still in position A? Does your mind tell you that the belief is true? If the answers to these questions are negative, go back and retake the steps.

CHAPTER 5: PRODUCTIVITY AND TIME MANAGEMENT

Time is perhaps the most valuable resource available to an entrepreneur or business owner. Indeed, the value of time is perceptible and can be appreciated in the popular phrase "time is money." After all, we have only 24 hours in a day to do all that we have to do. For entrepreneurs, especially those who have reached quite a remarkable stage in their business, the length of the day seems increasingly shorter; it is common to see these entrepreneurs struggle with managing time effectively to carry out their daily business activities.

As a business owner, you are your own boss. While this may sound exhilarating, it also means that you have to shoulder the brunt of the responsibilities at the workplace. You have to create and attend meetings, make marketing plans, create an effective budget, set up devices to monitor your sales, engage in networking, and so on. Honestly, all of these tasks could be quite daunting. To come anywhere close to achieving success in your business, you need to manage resources appropriately, especially the resource of time. Since time is not negotiable and cannot be purchased at will, optimizing every passing second of the day is key to achieving success. This especially applies to entrepreneurs who have just started their business or those who are looking to scale their business up. However, notwithstanding your business level or growth, you'd always need to manage your time as efficiently as possible.

It may be impossible or unthinkable to create time, but it is possible to create and develop attitudes that are geared toward ensuring that you make the best use of your time. Perhaps this metaphorical anecdote will help you to understand this point better: A professor once held an empty glass jar and began to fill it with golf balls. He filled the jar to the brim with golf balls, and then asked his students, "Is the jar full?" They responded, "Yes," in unison. Then, the professor picked up small stones and began to throw them into the spaces between the golf balls. When the jar seemed full and could no longer take more stones, he asked his students again if the jar was full, and again they answered in the affirmative. The professor then started to fill the spaces between the golf balls and stones with sand. When the jar could no longer take in more sand, he asked the students for the third time if the jar was full. The students, now obviously confused as to what to answer, kept quiet. The professor then got hold of a water bottle, uncovered it, and started to pour its content into the jar. Again, he filled the jar to the brim.

The lesson to learn in this short story is that time is like the professor's empty jar, containing nothing. The jar represents the total time you have per day – 24 hours. The contents of the jar represent the activities you may spend your time on during the day. The golf balls represent the most important activities you may engage in, the ones that move you towards achieving your goals. They are the big hitters, they have the greatest impact on your set goals and objectives and rank first on your list of priorities. The stones are activities that are both urgent and important, but that does not impact your goals significantly. If left unchecked, these activities can easily take up all of your days, leaving you with no time left to spend on your goals. The sand is an urgent activity that is not very important. You can leave these tasks for after you are done with your urgent and important tasks. The water represents the fact that you must reserve time to spend with family and friends. This should be time to unwind, relax, and reflect on everything you have done so far.

In order to maximize our time and get more done, we must start to plan our activities as and when we mean to do them. By planning, we can stack up activities in the future, so we take them on one after another as time goes on. NLP can help you plan better by making you work your plan from the future to the present. The NLP technique that helps you achieve this is called the timeline therapy. NLP Timeline therapy allows us to start our journey from the future so that we can assume better internal states while we work back to the present. When in the present, we can also work our plan forward, so as to ensure its feasibility. A major advantage of working from the future is that it allows us to be motivated enough to see the plan through to the end, which we are less likely to do when we begin from the present. So how exactly do we start to work from the future? The following exercise should show us how:

1. Sit in a comfortable place. Imagine that the future is in front of you and that it is a colorful triangle that keeps expanding. Imagine that your past is a triangle, positioned behind you. For the next few minutes, think of how you want your future to be and what you would be required to do to achieve that future.

2. Now place yourself in that future and imagine that you are now living the life that you want. Notice what you can see, hear, and feel at that moment. Integrate yourself completely into that mental picture and enjoy every moment of the future.

3. Use the double dissociation technique to dissociate from the "you" in the future. Observe the version of yourself in the future and mention three things that have helped you get there.

4. Begin to move towards to present, but don't arrive at the present just yet. Ask yourself what you did to master the three things you did that took you to that future.

5. Now come to the present. Ask yourself what you can start doing now to develop and master the three factors that can take you to the future you want.

6. Imagine that you have already developed and mastered the three factors required to give you the future you want and imagine all the hurdles and challenges you had to go through to arrive at mastering them.

7. What advice can you take from your future self? See if the version of you that has conquered the present and moved to the future has any vital advice to offer you.

8. Now start from the present and move towards the future, taking with you all of the advice you just garnered from your future self.

9. Lastly, show appreciation by thanking yourself for making time to plan your future.

Sometimes, as an entrepreneur, we get caught in a web of options, many different pathways we can pick and choose from – such as choosing from a number of marketing ideas. This situation can be an effective time-waster, as time spent on deliberating and choosing from the multitude of options could be spent on other important things. There is an NLP technique that can help you decide and choose faster in situations such as this, thereby saving you valuable time. This technique is known as the NLP visual squash and can be incredibly helpful.

NLP Visual Squash Technique

The visual squash technique is a simple yet effective NLP technique useful in resolving an internal crisis, such as an inability to make up your mind about something. Here are the steps in the technique:

1. You are going to have to trim your options down to just two or take all of the options two at a time for this exercise.

2. Create a mental picture of each of the two contrasting options and hold each picture in hand.

3. Feel the image in each hand and try to find out the positive intention it is trying to fulfill. What are the options trying to do for you? Create a mental picture of each of the intentions behind the two options. Now replace the pictures you have in each hand with the new mental pictures of intentions you just created.

4. Create a mental picture of the combination of all of the positive intentions of the two original options. Imagine this mental picture hovering over both your hands.
5. With a clapping motion, add the contents of your left hand with those of your right hand, and merge (or squash) them with the mental picture hovering over your hands.
6. When you are ready, place the palms of your hands on your chest and let your body absorb the third mental picture.
7. When you feel you have experienced the change you are looking for, break state, and return to the present moment. You should now have one unmistakable option to deal with.
8. If you have another set of two options, repeat the exercise for them, and when you have one option at the end of the process, repeat the exercise for the final options to arrive at only one.

Everyone has a limited supply of time, energy, and focus. It is relatively easy to lose time, get low on energy, and have depleted focus; so it's best to use them prudently. This is why planning is so invaluable. It allows you to be aware of and make the best use of your resources. Here are some tips for managing your time, energy, and focus on improved productivity:

- Set priorities and handle your top priority tasks first. Remember the golf balls metaphor – know the activities that get you closer to your goals and dedicate most of your time to carrying them out.
- Engage in activities that can increase your energy and focus, such as exercise, meditation, and rest. It is useless spending time on activities if you don't have enough energy or attention to see them through. Aim not only to maximize your time but also to improve the quality of the time you spend on tasks.
- To make the best use of your time, you must be able to discern between the various times of the day. There are times

when we are energetic and can carry out the most difficult tasks of the day, there are times when it is best to handle only the less physically demanding activities, and there are other times when it is best to rest. You must know what time is best for what and act accordingly.

- Start early and finish early. The most productive times of the day span from early in the morning to dusk. Many of the exceptional entrepreneurs of the world have emphasized the need to start the day early and finish in time for a good, long sleep. Make this a habit, and you'll notice a surge in your productivity.
- One of the best qualities of successful entrepreneurs is they know when to outsource and delegate. Even if within your capabilities, you must not complete all available tasks; this eats your time away considerably. It is OK to delegate specific tasks to people who have the abilities to handle them and can do so at rates affordable by you.

CHAPTER 6: COMMUNICA-TION

Communication is, quite simply, interacting with yourself or other people. Effective communication is vital for gaining insight into other people's circumstances and can help to know the "why" behind their actions, behaviors, or attitudes. In the world of business, effective communication is required between an organization and its clients to make sales; this is external communication. The organization would also have to have an effective communication strategy in place between the individuals at the helm and other staff; this is known as internal communication. For a business to thrive and achieve high levels of success, it has to put in place mechanisms that ensure that both external and internal communication needs are met. Therefore, there is always a need to strive for better communication, as it not only leads to more customer participation but also brings about the rapport between members of staff, hence improving productivity.

Communication can be verbal as well as nonverbal, and a good grasp of both can go a long way to motivate employees, convince clients, and help make sales. The most important communication skills for an entrepreneur who wishes to succeed in the business world include:

- **Conversing**

  Engaging in a conversation is one of the simplest forms of communication and one we all do on a daily basis – perhaps this accounts for why the art of conversing has been largely underestimated. A simple yet effective conversation with an employee can help build rapport and get you in the know of hitherto hidden issues. Even a seemingly innocent conversation with a stranger can turn into an opportunity to make sales. As an entrepreneur, you must learn to converse in a friendly and calm manner.

- **Body language**

A large part of our daily communication is nonverbal. Therefore, you must get a grip on your body presentation. The posture you assume in a conversation matters a lot. Sit or stand straight up; keep your shoulders back and relaxed; keep your head high and look the person you're conversing with straight in the eye. Your body language decides to a great extent whether you would be in command of a room or be just another occupant.

- **Writing**

If you are going to make headway in business, you will need to possess a certain level of writing skill. You don't have to be an expert with a pen, but you do need to be direct and concise when transferring words to paper.

- **Presentation skills**

You can't escape having to present your ideas, business reports, innovation, or business pitch to a group of people within or outside your organization from time to time. The way you present has a direct impact on how people would react to your presentation. You must be concise, clear, confident, and poised during presentations.

- **Negotiation skills**

Everything in business is based on negotiation – getting a deal from investors, making sales, and even paying employees. As so much depends on negotiation, the more you hone your negotiation skills, the better you would be at making deals that are favorable to you.

- **Mediation skills**

Although you may not do much mediating as an entrepreneur, there are times when you need to step up and mediate between conflicting parties. It may be employees or co-investors who can't agree on something; your mediating skills can be applied to extinguish any spark before it becomes a wildfire.

- **Debating**

There is a difference between debating and arguing; the former requires that you respectfully bring out your opinions and ideas as opposed to other people's opinions. You may need to convince investors, employees, or cofounders that your idea works best in a particular situation; the way you handle the situation will determine what they make of your viewpoints.

- **Cross-platform messaging**

There are more communication platforms now than ever, ranging from SMS, emails and phone calls to instant messages and video calls. You must learn to use the appropriate communication platform to handle your messaging tasks at all times.

- **Listening**

Listening is one of the most vital communication skills. Active and effective listening can enhance your leadership, debating, mediation, negotiation, and conversing skills.

Mastery of all of these skills can make you a better entrepreneur and a better, more thoughtful individual overall. As with any skill, you need to practice these skills consistently until they become part of you. When you fail to invest your time into becoming a better communicator, you fall into the pool of the many entrepreneurs whose businesses are failing due to a lack of proper communication skills. Here are some effects of poor communication on the business of an entrepreneur:

- Low morale at the workplace: When there is poor communication between those at the headship of an organization and the ground staff, what follows is a general drop in morale. Reduced morale affects productivity negatively, and the situation goes through a downward spiral of negativity and dissatisfaction after that.

- High employee turnover: One of the manifestations of poor communication in the workplace is an increase in employee turnover. It is logical for employees to seek work elsewhere if they feel dissatisfied with the treatment they are receiving at their current job. High turnover rates are injurious to the finances of a company, as it costs money to replace employees continuously.

- Poor customer service: Poor communication affects customer service in two ways: One, the employees may not have adequate instruction as to the tenets of customer relations, and hence lack the knowledge to attend to customers properly. Two, customers may perceive the low morale at the organization and therefore, have an unpleasant buying experience.

- Health issues may begin to develop: Poor communication can cause dissatisfaction among workers. If an individual is left with virtually no way to de-stress, stress can accumulate quickly and lead to the development of chronic mental and physical health problems.

- Dissatisfaction among customers: It is a no-brainer that when morale is low, and customer service is poor, customers may begin to feel uneasy patronizing your company. Hence, they soon take their business dealings elsewhere. This costs you money, lots of it.

- Poor communication breeds arguments: With personnel uncertain about their roles or not communicating effectively with one another about what needs to be done and how it has to be done, it is likely for them to be caught up in destructive arguments. Once this becomes the order of the day, it becomes difficult to move the company forward.

Poor communication can quickly erode the personnel and financial structure of a business. For a business to thrive and achieve its set goals and objectives, especially in this highly competitive era, there has to be in place an effective system of communication that not only improves communication between the owners of an enterprise and employees but also helps the employees to communicate better among themselves. There are several methods of improving communication in NLP. Of these methods, creating rapport, improving your tone of voice, and using eye accessing cues are the three most commonly used to attain positive results. These methods will now be discussed further.

Creating and Building Rapport

Building rapport with clients, team members, and employees is an important step in learning to communicate better with them. When you are in rapport with an individual, the contrasts between you and the person are minimized while your similarities are emphasized. Rapport allows you to be in sync with a person you are communicating with and allows the conversation to flow smoothly. Rapport can happen naturally between people over time, as we tend to like people who are like us. However, it is also possible to consciously and deliberately build rapport with someone in a bid to communicate better with them. There are two common ways of building rapport with someone; matching & mirroring and matching a person's representational state.

i. Matching and Mirroring

Matching and mirroring are one of the most effective ways of building rapport with a person. It is done subtly, in a way that doesn't seem like you are mimicking or copying the person, as these might have the opposite effect on the person. While mirroring a person, you essentially try to reflect the person's body language back to them in a manner that seems natural and comfortable for the person. Generally, the purpose of matching and mirroring is to build rapport with a person without their noticing what you are doing. You can mirror a person physically or verbally to achieve positive outcomes.

a. Physical Mirroring

In physical mirroring, you mirror a person's body language (e.g. tilting of the head, crossing of the arms or legs), posture (slumping or in an upright position, facing forwards or facing sideways), gestures (like the person's hand gestures while talking), breathing (slow or quick), and voice (the person's tone of voice, the speed of their speech, their volume and pitch). All of this is done in a very subtle manner. For example, if a person you're communicating with sits and crosses their left leg over their right leg, you can mirror that by crossing your right leg over your left leg, as though the person we're looking into a mirror.

b. Verbal Mirroring

Verbal mirroring can be done by mirroring a person's tone of voice as well as their pitch and the speech of their speech. You could make this process even more effective by repeating the person's last few spoken words in your next sentence.

ii. Matching the Other Person's Representational State

A person's representational system is exposed by words that have a big I pact on what they are talking about. People who are visually oriented tend to react best to the way things look; auditory oriented people respond best to the way things sound, and kinesthetic people respond best to the way things feel. This is so because the way we express ourselves will always be biased towards the sensory modality we prefer (visual, auditory, kinesthetic, olfactory, and gustatory). Sometimes a person may mix more than one modality, but the person's preferred modality will have the biggest impact on the way the person expresses themselves.

When you sync your words to reflect the preferred sensory modality of a person you're communicating with, you would be able to build rapport more easily and faster than when you mismatch modalities. For example, when a person says, "I don't feel this thing is right," it is evident that this person favors the kinesthetic sensory modality. You could then respond by saying, "I feel the same too," using the kinesthetic modality. This is a good way to build rapport. If you wish to master this art, you must cast aside your own sensory preferences and deliberately evaluate people's words to find the sensory modalities they prefer.

- **Visual Language**

A person who favors the visual sensory modality often uses words such as "see, vision, envision, look, appear, picture, and show" to convey their messages. For example, a person may say:

"I don't see this plan coming along."

"This method appears to be working well."

"The future looks bright."

- **Auditory Language**

An individual who prefers the auditory sensory modality uses words that reflect the hearing sensation, such as sound, hear, say, and listen, to express themselves. They may say, for example:

"That sounds like a good idea."

"I paid attention to and listen carefully to your speech."

"I hear you."

- **Kinesthetic Language**

People who prefer the kinesthetic sensory modality use words such as feel, grasp, let go and hold on to express themselves. Here are some examples:

"I don't feel the need to let go of the methods we currently have on the ground."

"I'm struggling to grasp the lesson in his anecdote."

"I want to hold on to my practices for now."

You can always tweak your statements to reflect a person's preferred sensory modality to connect with the person on a deeper level and build a strong rapport. Again it must be emphasized that you should know your own sensory preferences and make appropriate adjustments so that you do not crossmatch your own preferences on another person's. In case you do not know your preferred representational system yet, you can simply think of something and evaluate your reaction to it. For example, if you think of the woods and you begin the recollect images of the woods as well as everything one might find in the woods, you can be sure that you are a visually-oriented person. If you don't really care how the woods look but are rather paying attention to the sounds therein, then you are an auditory oriented person. If you think of the woods and you begin to feel the sensations of walking in the woods, then you have the kinesthetic sensory modality as you dominant or preferred representational system.

Using Eye Accessing Cues

In NLP, eye accessing cues represent movements of the eyes in certain directions that indicate visual, auditory, or kinesthetic reasoning. People tend to move their eyes in various directions while talking, and, according to NLP, we can deduce what representational system the person is thinking in by carefully observing their eye movements. Just as you would use a torch to point in various directions when looking for something within your home, we use our eyes to "look" inside our minds for information we have stowed away. Depending on where the information is stored, we can use the visual, auditory, or kinesthetic torch you look into our minds. You may have found the accessing cues out for yourself when you asked people questions, and they moved their eyes in a certain direction. There are six directions in which the eyes may turn while trying to secure information. They are top right (for visual remembered images), middle right (audio remembered images), bottom right (during self-talk or while making calculations), top left (visual constructed images), middle left (audio constructed images), and bottom left (tactile images) (see figure 6.1).

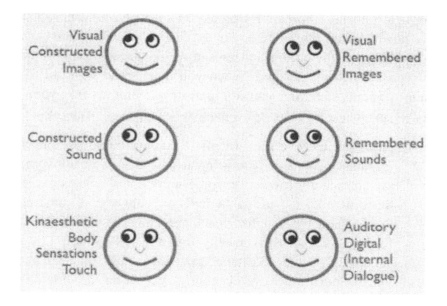

Table 6.1: Eye accessing cues

You need to keep this image in your head use it when you are in a conversation with someone. A good way to remember this image is to put yourself in the shoes of the observed person. When you look to the top right, you are trying to remember visual images because "remember" and "right" both begin with an "r." For example, if someone were to ask where you live, your eyes should move to the top right, because you are trying to remember the picture of the place you are living in. However, if you are asked to talk about your dream house, your eyes would probably look to the top left, because you are trying to construct images of your dream house.

In the same vein, if you're asked what your best friend's voice is like, you would look to the middle right as you are attempting to remember your best friend's voice. If you are asked how you would like your dream woman to sound, then your eyes would move to the middle left because you are trying to construct a voice you probably have never heard before. If you are asked how your breakfast tasted, you will look to the bottom left as you would be attempting to bring the taste back to the surface. When you understand what all of the eye movements stand for, you can then start to employ it in your day to day conversations. Here are some tips to help you through:

- Although the eye movements, as described above hold true for most people, it is worthy to note that these movements are completely revered in some individuals. For example, in these people, the top right may indicate visual constructed images and top left for visual remembered images, and so forth. This reversal is usually found in left-handed individuals, though not all left-handed people are like this. So, before you set out to use eye accessing cues in an individual, first ask that individual a question to which you already know the answer. Use the result you obtain from that test question to form your conclusions about that person's eye movements.

- It is possible that a person you are conversing with answers to your questions without moving their eyes to either side and keeping them fixed in the middle. This usually happens when the answer to a question lies in the person's short-term memory, and they don't need to think much before providing it; for example, "How old are you?"
- You must be as concise and straightforward as possible while searching for eye accessing cues. Avoid questions that may trigger extra and unnecessary thought patterns in people. Keep the questions straightforward and clean. For example, if you want to know the color of a person's apron, simply ask, "What color is your apron?" This would elicit a simple visual response. But, if you say, "Can you tell me what color your apron is?" You may not get a straight visual response, because the question "Can I?" may trigger self-talk within the person and cause them to look to the bottom right. This might be confusing.

A. Improving your Tone of Voice

Your tone of voice has a direct effect on your message and how people respond to it. When you increase your tone of voice, you sound better, and people are more willing to respond to you in a positive way. There are two common methods of carrying out this exercise. As with all exercises, you must practice these exercises regularly to master them and improve your tone of voice significantly fully.

Exercise 1

- With your preferred hand, press on your nose and say the word "nose."
- Continue to say the word until you feel that your nose is vibrating.
- Repeat this exercise with your throat while saying the word "throat."

- Then repeat the exercise on your chest while saying the word "chest."
- Notice the contrast between the sounds of different words.

Exercise 2

- Take a deep breath in.
- Open your mouth wide and say the letter "r" with a high tone. Prolong the pronunciation while reducing your tone gradually until you run out of breath.
- Do this ten more times.
- Again take a deep breath in.
- Say "ou" (you without the letter y) with a low pitch. Prolong it while increasing your tone of voice gradually until you can no longer increase your tone any further.
- Do this ten more times.

CHAPTER 7: NEGOTIATION AND SALES

In business, the most important thing is making sales. But sometimes it is also the hardest thing to do, due to the myriad of reasons why customers just won't buy our products and services. It could be that they don't need the product at the time of our advertising it, they may find that the price is too high for the value of the product, or the product may simply not be right for them. Whatever may be their reason, it is clear that sometimes selling a product or service in exchange for money is a Herculean task. But there are always ways around things with NLP. In NLP, a lot of emphasis is put on one's state of mind, as it has the potential to impact on a person's outlook and behavior, and hence, the response one gets from customers. So many of us had bought products in the past which, when we got home and evaluated, we decided we're not good value for our money and that we didn't really need or even want it. But then, why did we buy it in the first place? The salesperson! They just weren't prepared to let us go without having their product, and due to whatever reasons we could give ourselves, we ended up buying a product we may never use. Such is the power of negotiation in business.

Just as location is important when it comes to real estate, your state of mind is most important when it comes to sales. Do you believe you can sell your product? Do you think that your product or service is providing any sort of solution? Do you think your price is appropriate for the value your product promises? You need to answer all of these questions and be poised to make the customer understand why they need to make a purchase.

No matter what you are selling you must expect that some people will make objections. They will blame the color, price, and structure of your product, or liken it to a product they bought in the past that failed. You must be prepared for these objections and know how to respond to them. You could even use NLP to bring up the objections yourself before the customer does, in order to stop them in their tracks and leave them with no attacking potential. You could say, for instance, "Some say this security device is too costly, but what is the price of making sure you and your family are safe? Is this price higher than the value you place on their lives?" By bringing up a possible objection to the price of your product, you halt any thought processes in the customer in that direction and focus their thoughts instead on the value of their lives and those of their families. This is called a redirection technique. You could also use the redirection technique in another way.

Say you want to sell a car to a customer who would rather have another (that you don't currently have), you could liken their attitude to a weak or ineffectual state, such that they start to dissociate themselves from that attitude and come closer to making a purchase. For example, "Sorry, my friend, if I appear a little blunt, I had this customer some moments ago who just wasn't prepared to buy anything. He complained about everything, like the price of the vehicle, the color, even the tires, but what he should be complaining about really is his wife's grip on his collar. He simply didn't want to buy a car his wife wouldn't like. Now, tell me what manner of slavery that is, when you cannot even buy things because you want to. Sorry for taking your time, my friend, what brand would you WANT?" By bringing up a story of a (fictitious) customer whose wife apparently controlled his buying habits, your client immediately starts to dissociate himself from the other man and tries to act differently.

Negotiation is all about making rapport with your customers. While in deep rapport, you can influence the customer's decision and swag it in your direction. Inculcate the rapport skills we discussed in the previous chapter into your negotiation system and see a surge in your results. In addition to the rapport techniques we have learned, here are some tips to help you negotiate better and make sales:

- Try to establish a situation where everybody wins. Customers often see negotiation as a win or lose situation, where they stand against you in a heated contest. With this mindset, they find it difficult to come to terms with your proposition as they see the whole negotiation process as a competition. You need to reframe the situation and turn it to a win-win scenario by making the customer see the problems they would be solved if they purchased your product or service.

- Refrain from making counters claims. When a customer raises valid objections to tour products, do not immediately start attacking them or telling them why their opinions don't hold water. Instead, listen to them carefully, even agree with them on some fronts, and turn their arguments to your favor. For example, when a male client tells you a certain color is not for men, tell them, "Yes, traditionally this color is deemed not suitable for men, but out of the last ten customers who purchased this product, six of them were men. Maybe it's high time men tried something different."

- Learn useful metaphors and hypothetical situations you can use to sway customers in your direction. From time to time in a negotiation, bring up a hypothetical situation in which your product or service could be used to great effect. Make them understand why your service is the best option in that situation, and why they must not allow an adverse situation to happen.

- Have a handful of useful facts ready every time younger negotiating with a client. Make sure to poke holes in your client's defenses by bringing up indisputable facts that they just can't ignore. For example, "Why do you think the rich hardly have any cases of theft or burglary? It's because they have resorted to using the best security mechanisms available, however expensive they come." Sound authoritative, but not sarcastic or disrespectful. Use a commanding tone, but also be gentle and wise, and always wear a true smile.

CONCLUSION

Since its introduction in the 1970s by Richard Bandler and John Grinder, neurolinguistic programming has been used by many to improve the quality of their lives or that of the lives of other people. Perhaps the group of people who have utilized the principles and concepts of NLP to greatest effect is entrepreneurs, who, in the ever-demanding world of business, need to be perpetually sound physically and mentally. Many of the problems bedeviling entrepreneurs and impeding their progress, such as poor time management skills, bad decision making, low self-confidence, and poor communication can be easily remedied with NLP techniques. These NLP techniques have been created and developed over time to solve the multitudes of challenges the contemporary entrepreneur faces, such as are listed above. While some of these techniques were created and structured by the founding fathers of NLP, some others have been developed by NLP enthusiasts, psychotherapy experts, psychologists, and counselors to meet the psychological needs of their patients or clients. Not all NLP techniques are focused on effecting therapy; some are geared towards making an already sound mind, even firmer and more resilient. Others have been specifically designed to allow people to achieve the successes that exceptional individuals have experienced, by modeling the skills and toolset those exceptional people have utilized to their benefit.

Modeling is one of the earliest and most practiced NLP techniques. It allows you to fashion your life and your business after those of truly remarkable people who have achieved the goals you wish to attain. Through modeling, the founding fathers of NLP have themselves been able to create and develop techniques by studying the lives and works of exceptional psychotherapists, such as Milton Erickson and Satir. The works of these people have formed the larger part of what we practice as NLP today.

To achieve any success as an entrepreneur, it is important that you first have a vision, then break that vision down into feasible, achievable goals, which you can start working to attain. Setting goals is a common concept among entrepreneurs, but, indeed, few entrepreneurs have come to grips with the knowledge of setting goals that are not only achievable, but whose impact on the central vision can be easily measured. There are many strategies and methods that you can employ to make your goals workable. Two of the commonest methods are the SMART and PURE acronyms, which, either used singly or in collaboration, can help you fashion goals that will move you towards your ultimate vision.

This book offers theoretical insight into many of the commonly practiced NLP concepts, gives exercises to aid in understanding these concepts, and provides tips, tricks, and recommendations on important subject matters, such as goal setting, self-esteem, confidence, self-appreciation, communication, negotiation, and making sales. Applying the exercises and tips offered herein is certain to plunge you into the success circle and expand your horizon. However, you should not expect this book to be a magic wand; you can simply wave at your challenges and make them disappear. You must put in an effort to practice the resources provided in this book so that you can understand and master them.

Our mind is the central processing unit' build it and you can get yourself across any realm. This book offers you a set of mind-building instructions. You only need to reach out, practice them and make them your constant companions.

Good luck!!!

Dear Entrepreneur,

As an independent author,

    and one-man operation

    - my marketing budget is next to zero.

As such, the only way

    I can get my books in front of valued customers

    is with reviews.

Unfortunately, I'm competing against authors and

    giant publishing companies

    with multi-million-dollar marketing teams.

These behemoths can afford

    to give away hundreds of free books

    to boost their ranking and success.

Which as much as I'd love to –

    I simply can't afford to do.

That's why your honest review

    will not only be invaluable to me,

    but also to other readers.

Yours sincerely,

Joel E. Winston

Further reading

Standing still is going backwards. If you have enjoyed this book and you want to keep improving your results and income as an Entrepreneur, check out the following title from the same author.

Stoicism for Entrepreneurs
How to model today's best entrepreneurs by using
the ancient stoic self-disciplined mindset
Joel E. Winston

Here is a tiny bit of what you´ll discover:

- **How to persevere even if the odds seem stacked against you** (page 61)
- How to deal with the obstacles you face as an entrepreneur (page 42)
- <u>One simple rule</u> to help you decide where to <u>put your energy and focus</u> (page 60)
- How to raise your Self-Confidence as an entrepreneur (page 65)
- The No.1 method for continuous self-improvement in only 20 minutes a day (page 23)
- How to *increase your entrepreneurial motivation* and get more done in less time (page 57)
- To stoic way of turning adversity and setbacks into growth and improvements (page 59)
- How to **improve the relationship with your business partners** and get more business (page 70 and 82)
- How a holistic approach on life will benefit your business (page 83)

And much, much more.

Don´t waste your time and get more productive and learn how to deal with obstacles.

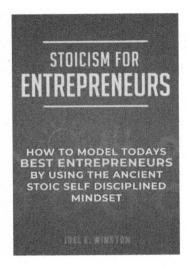

REFERENCES

1. Stipancic, M., Renner, W., Schutz P., Dond, R. (2009). Effects of Neuro-Linguistic Psychotherapy on Psychological Difficulties and Perceived Quality of Life. *J. Counselling and Psychotherapy Research.* https://doi.org/10.1080/14733140903225240
2. Zaharia, C., Reiner, M., Schutz, P. (2015). Evidence-Based Neuro-Linguistic Psychotherapy: A Meta-Analysis. *J. Psychiatria Danubina.* Vol. 27, No. 4, pages 355–363.
3. Rubino, J. (n.d.). The Impact of Lacking Self-esteem on Business Professionals. Retrieved from https://bodymindinstitute.com/the-impact-of-lacking-self-esteem-on-business-professionals/ [28 June 2019].

Made in the USA
Coppell, TX
01 July 2020